ON OUR KNEES
AND IN HIS ARMS

Foundations OF THE Faith

The Lord's Prayer

ON OUR KNEES

AND IN HIS ARMS

Peter Lewis

MOODY PRESS

CHICAGO

ISBN: 0-8024-3051-1

1 3 5 7 9 10 8 6 4 2

Printed in the United States of America

For my mother,
Winifred Lewis of Nantyglo, South Wales,
who first taught me to pray

CONTENTS

Part Three: "Give Us Today Our Daily Bread"

Part Four: "Forgive Us Our Debts As We Also Have Forgiven Our Debtors"

Part Five: "And Lead Us Not into Temptation, But Deliver Us from the Evil One"

Part Six: "For Yours Is the Kingdom and the Power and the Glory Forever. Amen"

PREFACE

$\mathcal{A}$ few years ago during a visit to Chicago, I toured the Sears Tower, a soaring skyscraper that seems to reach up over the city and to the sky. It's so tall that on some rainy days its top is literally in the clouds. But when skies are clear, the view from the top toward Lake Michigan and the other big Chicago loop buildings is inspiring. I like to think of prayer as a kind of skyscraper. It quite literally reaches beyond the skies—and gets there! It rises above the landscape while still being firmly grounded in it. It helps us to see the scene from a different perspective and enables us to respond to the needs around us with more perception and wisdom and effectiveness than we would otherwise have.

Like the skyscraper of a modern city, prayer in today's world is an engaged relevance, not an engaging irrelevance. This is a book about a great prayer and the truths that are the firm foundation of all prayer. It is not about prayer in general, nor is reading it praying! Yet it may be an elevator in the building of a prayer life that will help the reader to gain new heights as he or she prays to our Father in heaven.

The genius of the prayer Jesus gave to His disciples —the Lord's Prayer—lies chiefly in this: It contains all the main elements of prayer in a few lines. Each of these elements can be built upon as we meditate and pray. In this prayer we have God's character and His kingdom, His concern for others, and His care for ourselves. In it He shows concern for our spiritual warfare and declares our certain victory. That is why, in my view, such a short prayer requires such a long book as this and much thought by all of us who may pray it often.

I would like to thank the publishers of this American edition, Moody Press, and in particular James Bell, who included the book as part of Moody's Foundations of the Faith series. Jim also prepared the accompanying Review and Study Guide, which will help you to apply the truths of this prayer to your life. As ever, Jim Vincent has edited my original text with skill and sensitivity.

I record with gratitude and joy the love and support of my wife, Valerie, whose prayer life goes far in strengthening and sustaining me. Finally, I would like to record my love to and gratitude for the elders and members of the Cornerstone Church: "The boundary lines have fallen for me in pleasant places; surely I have a delightful inheritance" (Psalm 16:6). For almost thirty years I have enjoyed my ministry at the Cornerstone Church here in Nottingham, England.

INTRODUCTION:
WHY PRAY?

*I*t was a strange sight: a blind boy flying a kite with his father's help. A friend of the family watching dared to ask him a question, "What do you get out of this when you can't see the kite?" The answer was simple enough. "I can't see it but I can feel the pull," the boy replied.

Christians might make a similar reply to the questions, "Why pray to a God you can't see? Why put so much effort into an exercise so unquantifiable?" The answer might well be, "I can't see what's happening but I can feel the pull." It's true, I know, that often in the matter of a steady, faithful, disciplined prayer life we think more in terms of "push" than "pull." And so the question suggests itself, "Why pray?" As we prepare to study Jesus' magnificent prayer that we call "The Lord's Prayer," it's important that we answer that question.

The first and sufficient reason why we should pray is because God commands it. God would not tell us to do a meaningless act. He puts meaning into life, not futility. He would not tell us to do something which would waste our time and make a mockery of faith and obedience. If God tells us to pray, then prayer has its value and point from Him. His promise is its rationale and His power is its potential.

God repeatedly encourages us to pray, to honor His dominion, to seek His face, to discover His will, and to enlist His help. He has made us for Himself and prayer is an essential expression of that. We were made to pray. In prayer we assert the uniqueness of our humanity, which is made to relate to God. We became a fallen race and futility entered our world, but prayer—believing prayer and prayer in response to the call of God—is a step away from futility towards fulfillment. Prayer always brings me a little closer to God, whether I feel it so or not. Even if I do not feel anything has been achieved, God does.

In Matthew 6, just before He presented what we call the Lord's Prayer, Jesus said twice "When you pray" (vv. 6–7). Not "If you pray" but "When you pray." Later, with characteristic understanding that "the spirit is willing but the body is weak," (Matthew 26:41) Jesus told His followers a parable "to show them that they should always pray and not give up" (Luke 18:1). Above all else in prayer they were to keep on asking . . . seeking . . . knocking (Luke 11:9). The present continuous tense is repeatedly used for the Holy Spirit, whose presence and power would characterize life in the kingdom of God.

Second, we should pray because God is glorified in it. Nothing glorifies God quite like prayer. No one shares the glory with Him in this. Prayer begins as it ends, recognizing that His is "the kingdom, and the power, and the glory" (Matthew 6:13 NASB). Prayer gives God the glory of all His attributes or characteristics. It gives Him the glory of His *omniscience* (the word means all knowing, all seeing) in addressing Him. It gives Him the glory of His *omnipotence* (all powerfulness) and His *goodness* in seeking His help. It gives Him the glory of His *holiness* in making confession, of His *wisdom* in seeking guidance, and of His *mercy, grace,* and *love* in praise and thanksgiving. Nothing substitutes for prayer; it has its own unique part to play in honoring God.

Third, we should pray because people need our prayers. Prayer is an activity of care, a sign of love when we take it upon ourselves to pray regularly for someone. It involves us in that person's life as a partner and friend. The self-contained life knows little of love, but love opens us up to share other people's burdens and minister to others' needs; to become vulnerable, yes, but also to become an open channel for God through which He can pour His grace into needy lives.

It is a striking fact that the apostle Paul, who knew Christ's presence in His ministry with much unction and power, notwithstanding pleaded again and again for the prayers of His young churches: "Pray also for me, that whenever I open my mouth, words may be given me so that I will fearlessly make known the mystery of the gospel, for which I am an ambassador in chains. Pray that I may declare it fearlessly, as I should" (Ephesians 6:19–20).

If Paul needed prayer from people like ourselves in those early churches, surely there are others whom we know in ministry at home or abroad, sometimes in the hard places of the earth, with few securities and even fewer comforts who need the defense of our prayers, the assistance of our prayers, and quite simply the love of our prayers. (See Colossians 4:3; 1 Thessalonians 5:25–26.)

The fourth reason we should pray is because we change as we pray. During prayer, we become more aware of God as central to everything, the key to everything, and concerned about everything. This perception changes our attitude and approach in subtle ways. We become more dependent upon God, realizing our weakness, our inadequacy, and the danger of our own unchecked wisdom and willfulness. As we struggle with these things we become more conformed to God: to His nature, His will, and His ways. Richard Foster in his *Celebration of Discipline* writes: "To pray is to change. Prayer is the central avenue God uses to transform us."[1]

We may often struggle to pray, to submit to its disciplines, to respond to its calls. We may consequently feel we are no better after than before, no nearer our goals nor God's. But that is just not true. The promises given to prayer were not given to extraordinary practitioners but to very ordinary believers. Prayer changes things, and the first thing it changes is us! Though we do not see it, we grow as we pray.

Fifth, we should pray because things change as we pray. The English archbishop William Temple once said, "People tell me that answers to prayer are merely coincidences. I can only reply that when I pray coincidences happen and when I stop praying they stop happening."

One of the most dramatic answers to prayer was given to a church I know in Dunstable, England. A series of brutal attacks and rapes were carried out in the area by a criminal who came to be known as "the Fox" in the popular press because of his skill in evading the police.

Eventually this local church held special prayer meetings for the capture of the criminal; they prayed specifically, forcefully, persistently. Soon afterward "the Fox" was captured, and a picture appeared in the papers of the criminal handcuffed between two policemen. Both policemen were members of that same praying church. Was that God's comment on "coincidence"?

Sixth, we should pray because Jesus prayed. If the Son of God needed to pray in His earthly life, how much more do we! His prayer life focused His sense of obedience and dependence (John 5:19, 30), and He prayed on special occasions as well, such as at His baptism, before choosing the twelve disciples, before the Transfiguration, and before His passion. The prayer life of our Lord Jesus continues in a new mode in His exalted life. The one who gave us the Lord's Prayer always lives to intercede for us. He is the Great Pray-er.

NOTE

1. Richard Foster, *Celebration of Discipline,* rev. ed. (San Francisco: Harper & Row, 1988), 33.

PART ONE

"OUR FATHER IN HEAVEN,
HALLOWED BE YOUR NAME"

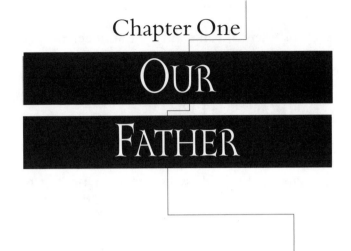

Chapter One

OUR

FATHER

The first two words of this prayer are a celebration— a celebration of God! We celebrate a relationship with Him; a relationship that has in it the genius and glory of every other relationship: the pride of the parent, the security of the child, the confidence of friends, the pleasure of lovers, and the joy of bride and groom. God has many names and titles to show His place in that relationship: King, Master, Shepherd, Friend, etc. But "Father" goes beyond them all and is the most profound of them all, indicating our ultimate identity and our supreme privilege, our dignity and our duty. The apostle John wrote, "How great is the love the Father has lavished on us, that we should be called children of God!" (1 John 3:1).

God is our *Father;* we belong to Him. This one truth tells us who we are and why we are; it tells us how we must live and how we may die; and it challenges us and comforts us. It is now the first and most important truth about our relationship with God. We may not understand His essential being but we can understand His character and His relationship to us with its commitment, authority, and love. He is not, after all, "the unknown God"; in Jesus Christ His Son He has become our Father-God (John 1:12).

I do not take this name or title of God in a gender-specific way. Take every characteristic of good parenthood, from father and mother, take every fond experience and valued association and raise it to the highest degree, and you will have glimpsed the character of God, the Father and Mother of us all, the heavenly parent. This divine Parent is strong and gentle, firm and tender, slow to anger, and quick to forgive, encourage, and embrace.

My first memory is of my mother's smile, her eyes shining with love and pleasure. I had done nothing to earn it (nor could I at two years old!), nor did I need to do so. It was a love called by the old theologians *complacere,* literally "complacent," but in the original sense of "resting on" with delight; that is, a love that simply delighted in its object. That is principally the love with which the Father loves the Son. But the wonder of grace is that when we are "in Christ" we ourselves become sharers of that love. Jesus revealed that in His prayer to His Father in John 17: "I have made you known to them, and will continue to make you known in order that the love you have for me may be in them" (v. 26).

It is often hard for us to think that God might love us in this simple, ungrudging, delighted way, but in heaven and thereafter it will be evidently the case. Yet we are no less "in Christ" now than then. We are unworthy and sinners still, who often grieve and even anger Him, so how can it be that in Christ God sees us with joy and satisfaction? The explanation lies in this crucial phrase "in Christ," which recurs so often in the New Testament to describe the believer's standing before God, his place in the Father's plan and in the representative work of Christ.

Christ has become for us "wisdom from God—that is, our righteousness, holiness and redemption"(1 Corinthians 1:30). Consequently, "in Him" we are complete: redeemed for God, forgiven by God, and destined by God for "the praise of his glorious grace." (See Ephesians 1:4–12, and especially v. 6.) So the love of God for us is one with the love the Father has for the Son (note John 17:23), and on that secure love we can build better, stronger Christian lives.

My father, as well as my mother, helped me to understand the various facets of love. He was a man of immense integrity and real devotion, though less able to express his affections in words than my mother. He was a quiet, placid though strong-minded character with considerable gifts in music; a solid and reliable support to those who depended on him. He also embodied the saying that the best gift a father can ever give his children is to love their mother. Sadly without Christian faith himself, he yet inherited from a godly father an unshakable sense of right and wrong. If ever I had robbed a bank and he came to know of it, I have no doubt he would have marched me to the prison cell in person. But he would also have visited me every day! Consequently my respect for my father was as great as my love; indeed to this day I regard respect as a quality of love (that is, as giving quality to it), even if it is not exactly a condition of love. We sometimes have to go on loving even where we have lost respect for the loved one; but then, love, admirable as it may be, is weakened by the very object to which it goes out.

We hear too little of respect these days, in or out of the home; and even in Christian circles reverence is not an attitude much cultivated or perhaps even understood. When did you last hear or speak or even think of someone being "God-fearing"? Yet the fear of God is a concept as biblical as the fatherhood of God. Of course such "fear" is not base or threatening. It is not terror or insecurity we are speaking of here, but reverence, respect, a recognition of His righteousness, truth, and justice, which will not compromise and which does not surrender its own character when it seeks to elevate ours.

Sometimes when I was in flight from my father the only safe place in the whole wide world was behind my mother. But where shall one go to escape the wrath of God? Only to God Himself, whose mercies are more than our sins, whose love has honored His justice once and for all, and who is always ready to forgive those who are truly sorry. No child rubbing his tear-stained face into his father's (as my children have done in years gone by) was ever more assured of complete forgiveness and every tender demonstration of acceptance and love, than the repentant believer turning from wrongdoing to his Father in heaven. No one delights in mercy more than "the Father of compassion and the God of all comfort" (2 Corinthians 1:3).

I realize, of course, that not everyone has good associations with the concept of a father. In our sinful, spoiled world of selfishness, of cruelty and fractured relationships, even the father-child relationship has been betrayed and broken in many cases. And in a world of wars and sickness and sudden death, many children have lost their birthright and been cheated of a parent. Yet in countless lives, the earthly relationship has been in some small way the mirror of the divine.

God may be for you the Father you never had. You may have grown up with an aching gap in your life. But God knew; He drew you to Himself, He led you to one who is the Son of God by nature that you might become a child of God by grace. He adopted you. By new birth you carry His name. Now, "born of the Spirit, washed in the blood," you and I have become "partakers of the divine nature" (2 Peter 1:4 NASB), for He dwells in us and will be with us. God is shaping you in the beauty of holiness to make you like Himself. You have a Father now— you are not cheated.

He may be for others a Father in stark contrast to their earthly parent. Perhaps it has been an effort for you to call him "Father" because of past associations with an unworthy or unloving father. God stands in contrast to many earthly parents. They were brutal; He is gentle. They were indifferent; He is committed. They were foolish; He is wise. They were distant; He has no inhibitions. He is the Father you always wanted, and you are His wanted child. The knowledge of this lies at the heart of our peace, and the celebration of this is the crowning glory of our prayers, said or sung.

Chapter Two

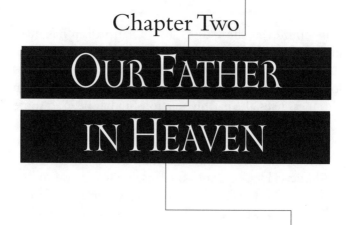

OUR FATHER IN HEAVEN

*I*n his book *Knowing God,* J. I. Packer warns us that Christians today largely lack a true appreciation of the majesty of God, adding: "and that is one reason why our faith is so feeble and our worship so flabby. We are modern men, and modern men, though they cherish great thoughts of man, have as a rule small thoughts of God."[1]

One reason, perhaps, why the transcendence of God has less attraction for the contemporary mind, even of believers, is that in spite of our great thoughts about ourselves we feel increasingly lost in our ever-expanding universe, and increasingly insignificant in our technological society. We constantly need affirmation and attention, a place of our own in the scheme of things. Much of our modern world dwarfs us, towering over us like our skyscrapers and telling us we don't matter. In our village communities of the past we had identities, but in the modern industrial and technological world we have only an identity crisis. We feel anonymous and insecure. We are crushed by the greatness of what is created, and we do not want to think too much of a power which towers even above that.

However, we do not need to regard God's greatness as a challenge to our meaningfulness, for God Himself has long ago brought them together: "For this is what the high and lofty One says—he who lives forever, whose name is holy: 'I live in a high and holy place, but also with him who is contrite and lowly in spirit, to revive the spirit of the lowly and to revive the heart of the contrite'" (Isaiah 57:15). And here our Lord Jesus Himself tells us that the first and last, the supreme and the definitive truth about us is that we have a Father who is in heaven. And the more we consider those two things *together,* the greater will be our joy and peace in believing.

Brilliant physicist Stephen Hawking concludes from modern science's measurements of the size of the physical universe: "We are such insignificant creatures on a minor planet of a very average star in the outer suburbs of one of a hundred thousand million galaxies ... that it is difficult to believe in a God that would care about us or even notice our existence."[2] But this experience of our littleness and creation's vastness is not new at all. Three thousand years ago the psalmist wrote of it—but with a very different conclusion.

> O Lord, our Lord, how majestic is your name in all the earth!
> You have set your glory above the heavens.
> When I consider your heavens, the work of your fingers,
> the moon and stars, which you have set in place,
> what is man that you are mindful of him,
> the son of man that you care for him?

> You made him a little lower than the heavenly beings
> and crowned him with glory and honor. (Psalm 8:1, 3–5)

The psalmist might have known much less about creation than modern scientists, but he knew far more about God! The psalmist knew that creation is big, even if he didn't know just how big. He also knew that God is bigger, so much so that size to Him is irrelevant. (See Isaiah 40:10–14, 22, 26–31.) The God who is great in big things is even greater in small things—including His tender regard for us.

NOTES

1. J. I. Packer, *Knowing God* (Downers Grove, Ill.: InterVarsity, 1973), 73–74.
2. Michael White and John Gribben, *Stephen Hawking: A Life in Science* (London: Penguin, 1992), 166.

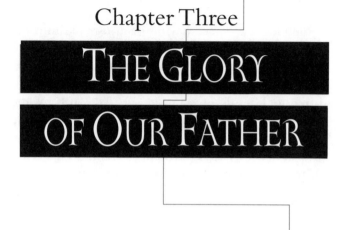

Chapter Three

THE GLORY
OF OUR FATHER

The Bible is full of God's glory and majesty, His transcendence and His sovereignty. And so we should reflect this awareness of Him in our prayer and praise. We should recall the "heavenliness" of God. "Our Father in heaven" has power and majesty, and we should recall His greatness and His glory.

These qualities became early lessons in the history of Israel, God's chosen people, and they are never lost or left behind in the ongoing biblical revelation concerning God. In the beginning He is there without beginning, the self-existent God (Genesis 1:1; Exodus 3:14), the Creator of the heavens and the earth. He is also distinct from His creation: in it yet above it, sustaining it yet transcending it. His creation cannot contain Him (1 Kings 8:27).

In a world of idolatry, the spirituality of God was carefully guarded, yet at times God manifested Himself on earth in a created glory, "the glory of the Lord." Even this was, properly speaking, indescribable. Moses, Aaron, and the elders of Israel, having been ushered into the presence of the Lord, could only speak of the splendor under His feet (Exodus 24:10). Moses alone was permitted to see God's "back" but not His "face," that is His retiring, not His full, glory (Exodus 33:23). Isaiah saw the fringe of God's glory, "the train of his robe" that filled the temple and brought the young prophet to his knees in terror and self-revulsion (Isaiah 6:1–5), and Ezekiel, who perhaps saw the most, could call what he witnessed only "the appearance of the likeness of the glory of the Lord," beautiful but fearful (Ezekiel 1:26–28).

God's majesty is as moral as it is mighty. The hymn writer rightly described God as "perfect in power, in love, and purity." Abraham knew the righteous God is "the Judge of all the earth"(Genesis 18:25). When these things are most deeply felt, at the near approach of God to His people, there is a sense of *awe* that overcomes the best of them. At the burning bush Moses "hid his face" because he was afraid to look on God (Exodus 3:6). At the foot of Sinai the people said to Moses, "Speak to us yourself and we will listen. But do not have God speak to us or we will die" (20:19). When Job at last felt God come near he said, "I despise myself and repent in dust and ashes," and young Isaiah cried out, "I am ruined" (Job 42:6; Isaiah 6:5); Ezekiel "fell facedown," and Daniel swooned and was drained of strength even to speak when God's angel, bearing but a reflected glory, approached him (Ezekiel 1:28; Daniel 10:8–9, 15–19). The glory of God shining from the face of the risen Christ, who is the image of the invisible God, blinded Saul of Tarsus, and when the apostle John saw it he recorded, "I fell at his feet as though dead"(Revelation 1:17).

It is right that we should approach with confidence our Father in heaven when we pray (see Hebrews 10:19). But it is also right that we should marvel at our privilege and even our safety in doing so! For the ancient Hebrew, the Holy of Holies was a frightening place, and for the modern Christian it is only because Jesus has gone there as our redeemer and mediator that it has become our eternal home.

Chapter Four

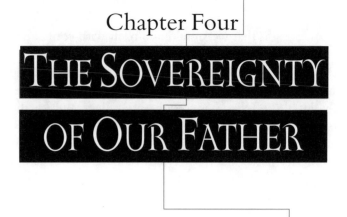

THE SOVEREIGNTY
OF OUR FATHER

*T*his God is God and there is no one beside Him. God Himself declares through Isaiah, "I am the Lord, and there is no other" (45:5). He is *eternal,* the aeons of creation are but passing moments to Him: "From everlasting to everlasting you are God" (Psalm 90:2). He is *omniscient,* seeing and knowing all that is, all that has been, and all that ever will be, planning and bringing to perfection all He has purposed (see Isaiah 46:8–10). No contradiction can finally defeat His plans for He is *omnipotent,* the Almighty God, who promises His people great and glorious things—which sometimes seem unlikely or lost in a world of disappointments—but who says when faith is low, "Is anything too hard for the Lord?" (Genesis 18:14).

The doctrine of God's sovereignty is given not to crush us but to comfort us. We may sometimes have problems with the doctrine, but we would have many more if He were not "the sovereign Lord." If He were only sovereign in heaven, what would be the point of praying this prayer on earth? If He were only sovereign in the church, who would help us in the world? But in fact He is the sovereign Lord, the Most High of whom we can say, "He is my refuge and my fortress, my God, in whom I trust" (Psalm 91:2). Others have their contacts in high places, but we have a Father in the highest place of all: big enough for all our problems, concerned enough for all our cares, and close enough to guide, protect, and reassure.

As we walk through life, problems meet us that dwarf us, and we are tempted to feel hopeless as well as helpless. Yet when we kneel to pray in full recognition of God's greatness, we see our problems themselves dwarfed before the God of all the earth, the sovereign and transcendent God—"our Father."

When I was a boy I was frequently bullied, being an excitable but nonaggressive type of child. Indeed I had little physical courage and went in daily dread of the village bullies at school and outside. Yet one day I walked through a gang of them without a qualm, smiling and nodding to one and another—and why? Only because my *father was with me,* strong enough and near enough to deal with any or all of them. Oddly, his presence turned their contempt into something like friendliness as they nodded back and said polite enough hellos. So with the knowledge of our Father in heaven we can meet life's "bullies"—its fears, frustrations, and failures; its sorrows and its losses—on new terms and with new resources.

Indeed our Father in heaven can turn those bullies to good, turning setbacks into stepping-stones, opponents into allies, losses into gains: "And we know that in all things God works for the good of those who love him, who have been called according to his purpose" (Romans 8:28).

Chapter Five

OUR

HOLY FATHER

*T*here is an extraordinary paradox in the two words *Holy Father:* they mean almost impossibly different things. The Hebrew word for *holy* is *quadosh,* a word whose root probably means cut, and the essential idea is that God is "cut off" from everything else; He is *different,* so different as to be immeasurably removed in His essential being from all other things.

How different is He from all things? They are created; He is uncreated. They are finite; He is infinite. They are (now) spoiled by sin; He is "too pure to look on evil" or to "tolerate wrong" (Habakkuk 1:13). Even unfallen angels bow in awe before the eternal mystery of God's "otherness," and the brightest and the best of His human children are, like the young Isaiah, staggered and threatened by His awe-full purity.

But if *holy* means *other, Father* means *like;* it carries overtures of similarity, of belonging, of identity. It was perhaps because Israel had to learn the lesson of Yahweh's holiness that it hesitated to call him "Father," certainly in the intimate sense of Jesus' Aramaic "Abba." He might be called Father to the nation (see Isaiah 63:15–16), but to domesticate or even personalize such a relationship in that way must have seemed shocking and presumptuous. But then Jesus came ...

Donald Guthrie in his *New Testament Theology* writes: "It is the idea of the Fatherhood of God which is most characteristic of New Testament teaching and especially of the teaching of Jesus."[1] The meaning and implication of that fatherhood is strikingly brought out in Jesus' use of "Abba" when addressing God. All Jewish children at home spoke this confident form of the name for their earthly fathers, and Jesus' earliest followers used this intimate form for their Father in heaven. (See Mark 14:36; Romans 8:15; Galatians 4:6.) "The Abba form," says Guthrie, "conveys a sense of intimacy and familiarity which introduced an entirely new factor into man's approach to God."[2]

This does not at all mean that God is less majestic, less exalted, less awesome than had been thought. It is not meant to lower God but to lift up ourselves. It is not that God is diminished, only that *we* are exalted. He is still "fearful in praises" (Exodus 15:11 KJV), but we are called to enter, with complete safety and confidence, that daunting glory which awes angels and would have destroyed sinners.

The writer to the Hebrews perfectly unites the reverence due to God with the confidence proper to sons and daughters when, in view of the whole priestly work of Jesus Christ, he urges his readers, "Let us then approach the throne of grace with confidence, so that we may receive mercy and find grace to help us in our time of need" (Hebrews 4:16). Later he amplifies:

> Therefore, brothers, since we have confidence to enter the Most Holy Place by the blood of Jesus, by a new and living way opened for us through the curtain, that is, his body, and since we have a great priest over the house of God, let us draw near ... in full assurance of faith, having our hearts sprinkled to cleanse us from a guilty conscience and having our bodies washed with pure water. (10:19–22)

No one who understands God, or the gospel, or themselves, will find strange the biblical stress on sin or the place of reverence and humility in true worship. In proportion, as we have exalted thoughts of God, we are likely to have lowly thoughts of ourselves; in proportion, as we understand His holiness and purity, we shall confess our sin and unworthiness to be called His sons and daughters, but, in proportion, as we understand His love and grace in the gospel, we shall accept His forgiveness and love, wear the robe and ring, and share the joy of the Father's house. (See Luke 15:22–24.)

I have never found this more movingly put than in the hymn by Thomas Binney:

> Eternal Light! Eternal Light!
> How pure the soul must be,
> When, placed within Thy searching sight,
> It shrinks not, but with calm delight
> Can live and look on Thee.
>
> O how shall I, whose native sphere
> Is dark, whose mind is dim,

Before th' Ineffable appear
And on my naked spirit bear
The uncreated dream?

There is a way for man to rise
To that sublime abode:
An offering and a sacrifice,
A Holy Spirit's energies,
An Advocate with God. [3]

NOTES

1. Donald Guthrie, *New Testament Theology* (Downers Grove, Ill.: InterVarsity, 1981), 80.
2. Ibid., 84.
3. Thomas Binney (1798–1874), "Eternal Light, Eternal Light." In public domain.

Chapter Six

A FATHER
WHO LOVES

$\mathcal{O}$ur Father" is also a Father of love. Anyone who imagines that the Old Testament presents only a God of wrath and that it was left to the New Testament writers to discover God's love shows a pretty woeful ignorance of both! From the start of the Old Testament, and increasingly throughout its books of law and prophecy, psalms and history, we are constantly shown that love is essential to God. Carl Henry writes: "Love is not accidental or incidental to God; it is an essential revelation of the divine nature, a fundamental and eternal perfection . . . it is the shaping principle of his creative and redeeming work!"[1]

If holy is *what* God is, love is *how* He is. Among the biblical writers no one soars higher in matters of doctrine than the apostle John. His gospel begins with one of the most sublime declarations of the person of Christ in the entire Scriptures. (See John 1:1–18.) Yet the same writer, in his first epistle, gives us an equally memorable doctrine of God the Father as light and life and truth and, above all, love: "God is love. Whoever lives in love lives in God, and God in him. . . . Whoever does not love does not know God, because God is love" (1 John 4:16, 8; see also 3:1 and 4:7–12).

Because He is love, we can trust Him, obey Him, and love Him in return without reserve and without conditions. It is His love which controls His power; it is His love which sets His goals and sustains His purposes of grace; it is His love which makes Him accessible to us in all His perfection.

Love is the first of six distinctly fatherly traits we will consider in the next six chapters, as we consider the address, "our Father." Love in God our Father is not only a resident quality but also an outgoing force. When we think of the word *love,* we often think of the idea of romance, and the word can easily become sentimental. But the essence of love at its highest is *self-giving.* This self-giving appears throughout the Scriptures; it characterizes the love of God for the world. It is, however, a self-giving love found upon grace, because when God gave Himself for us we were His enemies, not His friends, living in selfish rebellion, not seeking Him in racial repentance for reconciliation. As Paul explains:

> You see, at just the right time, when we were still powerless, Christ died for the ungodly. Very rarely will anyone die for a righteous man, though for a good man someone might possibly dare to die. But God demonstrates His own love for us in this: While we were still sinners, Christ died for us. (Romans 5:6–8)

This is precisely the extent of God's love and self-giving. When God the Father sent the Son into the world He did not stay behind, as it were, safe, invulnerable, uninvolved. In Jesus, God came. He was "Immanuel," God with us: God in the stable and the manger, God in the carpenter's shop, God on the Galilean road, and God on the cross of Calvary's hill. And while it was God the Son who became man and died for us, He was the point of vulnerability and pain for the whole Godhead. "For God so loved the world that *he gave* his one and only Son" (John 3:16, italics added). And when God gave up his own Son He did not give *someone else* to bear our sins: He gave Himself in the person of His beloved Son, for "God was reconciling the world to himself in Christ, not counting men's sins against them" (2 Corinthians 5:19).

Here is the infinite God, eternally self-sufficient in power and blessedness and glory. He did not have to create the universe or this world. Yet in His love and goodness He purposed to create our world and ourselves in it, and to create us, not as bits of nature but as unique beings, known by Him and made to know Him. This world was made for us in all its complexity, and we were made for Him in all our uniqueness (see Genesis 1:26–28). We were never meant to be lost in this world, anonymous in the great cosmos, dying without hope, leaving the world without knowing why we came into it.

But God's Word tells us that we fell as a race, and fell far and foully; sin entered our history and damaged our world. It became a world of conflict and fear and failure and despair, a world dominated by sin and death. For all its beauty there was a sickness at its heart, and for all our dignity there was a sickness in our heart too. Thus through-out our history we see war and exploitation and cruelty and disease and death.

Yet into this world God came. He did not have to come. He could have demolished the whole thing and started again; He could have crumpled it all up, tossed it into some celestial wastebasket and made a new race, one that would not rebel and corrupt His creation. But He did not. Through the long centuries He "suffered us" to go on in our ways. And often terrible ways they were too. And in that dark and primitive world He began the history of redemption: calling a man, Abraham; claiming a nation, Israel; and sending the prophets to teach the true faith in a world where our religions were often as debased as we. Finally, in the fullness of time, "God sent his Son, born of a woman," one utterly holy, entirely obedient human being, divine but also human, living the life that was demanded of us (Galatians 4:4–5).

Then the Son died the death that could have been demanded of us, the death sin deserved, bearing the wrath of God, pent up through the centuries of human sin. "God presented him as a sacrifice of atonement, [which would become effective in our lives] through faith in his blood. . . . He did this," Paul explains, "to demonstrate his justice at the present time, so as to be just and the one who justifies those who have faith in Jesus." (Romans 3:25, 26). John adds, "This is love: not that we loved God, but that he loved us and sent his Son as an atoning sacrifice for our sins" (1 John 4:10).

In the death of Christ we find the love of God. Father, Son, and Holy Spirit, in a holy conspiracy, achieved the best act of God in the worst act of humanity. There we learn what love is and see its highest demonstration. (Note, for example, John 15:12.) There we learn that love is not merely attitude but action, not simply sympathy but movement, and as we move out into our world in love we move out with God, coworkers with the Great Lover, and witness to all we meet that "God is love."

NOTE

1. Carl F. Henry, *God, Revelation and Authority,* vol. 6 (Waco, Tex.: Word, 1983), 341.

Chapter Seven

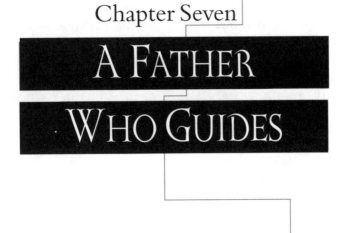

A FATHER
WHO GUIDES

$\mathscr{A}$s our Father, God has a plan for our lives. It's a plan drawn by a heavenly Father: perfect in love and wisdom. It is not a plan like a blueprint set out on a clean sheet of paper. It is one made in the full knowledge of the effects on each of us of the confusion, tragedy, injustice, and distortions of a fallen world. It is a secure plan, but drawn up with tears in prospect of the abused child, the battered mother, the wrecked career, and the widespread victims of disease, accident, and war. It is a battle plan that enlists us among the armies of light and truth, of love and peace, of faith and hope in a world of superstition and despair, in a world of the half-truth and the lie, a world of selfishness and cynicism.

God's plan will not fail, drawn by a love that will not give up and a sovereignty that will not be denied. (See John 6:37–40; Ephesians 1:11.) While drawn with tears, the plan also has been drawn with unquenchable joy by the God who knows the end of a thing from its beginning.

Meantime He leads His child through darkness and storm, sunshine and success, setback and sorrow—to victory. Hymn writer John Newman pictures God's unstoppable power:

> So long Thy pow'r hath blest me, sure it still
> Will lead me on
> O'er moor and fen o'er crag and torrent 'til
> The night is gone. [1]

On our knees and on our feet, making our decisions and keeping them, we can rely on a Father who guides us, who will correct or confirm our expectations, who educates us in His school and puts us to work in His world (we go to both at the same time!). The writer of Proverbs went to that school and sought to model his wisdom on God's and to teach his sons as God had taught him: "Trust in the Lord with all your heart and lean not on your own understanding; in all your ways acknowledge him, and he will make your paths straight" (Proverbs 3:5–6).

Sadly, Solomon found it easier to teach such wisdom than to practice it. (See 1 Kings 11:1–6.) When truth becomes theoretical we become philosophers instead of practitioners, and philosophers have been among the most foolish as well as the most wise of men. The wisdom of the Old Testament is a practical wisdom, a God-fearing obedience: Solomon himself knew this, writing, "The fear of the Lord is the beginning of wisdom" (Proverbs 9:10; see also 1:7).

Understand that God is concerned to guide us. He is

not content to be on the sidelines watching or at the end of our journey waiting. He has said clearly and firmly: "I will instruct you and teach you in the way you should go; I will counsel you and watch over you. Do not be like the horse or the mule, which have no understanding but must be controlled by bit and bridle or they will not come to you" (Psalm 32:8–9).

How often we let the pride and pressures of life control us; how often outside sources become the bit and bridle. Often God has to steer us, His children, who are supposed to listen, in just the same way as He has to steer others who are not His children and have no intention of going His way. God's guidance is a privilege that we can and should make much of, however complicated we find it. John White is absolutely right when he says:

> The heart and core of the guidance God gives is bound up in the personal relationship he wants to have with us ... He wants to guide me. He is interested in me, ... He doesn't say "O don't bother me now. I have the matters of the universe to look after. I have a new galaxy that I'm getting into place and it's rather tricky. Please don't come to me for guidance about something in the kitchen sink."[2]

However, just as God's concern is with every aspect of our lives, so our concern must be for His lordship over every aspect of our lives and for the will of God to be done in every part of those lives. Again White gives wise counsel:

> God is not interested in guiding us about just one choice. Suppose I say to an interior decorator: "Look at our dining room. It's a mess. Please do something about

it." But the interior decorator might respond, "Your dining room is a mess. But the problem is that your whole life is a mess. I can't fix the dining room without also dealing with everything that is around it. Give me the whole house to decorate. I'll do the job. But don't ask me to do the dining room alone."

When we come to God asking for guidance he says "Give me your life." That is his priority. He does not want to guide us about a specific issue alone. "You have that problem in your life," he says, "because you have not given to me the whole of your life."[3]

The most important thing in this difficult area of guidance, of decision making, of knowing God's will, is not so much the decisions we make but the spirit in which we make them. It's not our calculation but our consecration. If this is right then we may still make mistakes and we may still be led to testing times and experiences, but we can trust a sovereign God whose providence can recover us and redirect us, for "we know that in all things God works for the good of those who love him, who have been called according to his purpose" (Romans 8:28).

Often we have to proceed in life without knowing the next step or even the final (earthly!) goal. One man whose trust in the Lord led him to a great adventure was Abraham. He became father of many nations, but only because God became a Father to him and because he obeyed God's call: "Leave your country, your people and your father's household and go to the land I will show you" (Genesis 12:1; see also 17:4). Someone has said that when God called Abraham out from Ur of the Chaldees, "He did not know where he was going but he knew who he was going with!" This is what matters most for us all.

Sometimes the guiding hand and presence of our Father is hardest to discern in the delays of life, in its frustrating inactivity in sickness or unemployment. In the Bible of George Müller a marginal note was found beside Psalm 37:23 (KJV): "The steps of a good man are ordered of the Lord"—"and the stops too," Müller had added!

In the end our Father guides us and gets us to the points, more crucial perhaps than we know, where we play a critical part in His larger purposes, His master plan. And our part in all this is to walk in faith, in prayer, and, according to His Word, in common sense and with an ear for the wise counsel of friends. Then we can show the peace of a surrendered heart in safe hands.

NOTES

1. John Henry Newman (1801–1890), "Lead Kindly Light." In public domain.
2. John White, *The Race* (Downers Grove, Ill.: InterVarsity, 1984), 145, 147.
3. Ibid., 151–52.

Chapter Eight

A FATHER

WITH AUTHORITY

*I*t is, no doubt, a sign of our times that the first association with the word *Father* in Jesus' time is possibly the last we might make in our own. It is the concept
of authority. In the first century, almost universally, a
father had great authority over his children, even into
their adulthood and marriage. True, that authority must
have been often misdirected or abused. But in God we
have the best of fathers with the best of purposes directed
by the highest wisdom and the purest love.

In our own time the concept of authority has
become so devalued that it is largely regarded as out-of-
date and socially undesirable. We think that authority
interferes with individual growth and even individual
freedom. What for centuries was regarded as a vital good
is now regarded by many as an evil. Harry Blamires has
replied well to this:

The public mind in our generation has been confused and misled precisely by concealment of the fact that in religion, in education, in the life of society generally, it is authority that saves us from authoritarianism. It is respect for the central orthodoxies of law, culture and religion that alone preserves us from a multiplicity of intolerable petty authoritarianisms exercised by those who have the loudest voices, the strongest arms, or the most assertive egos.[1]

To repeat his assertion: "Authority saves us from authoritarianism." To recognize the authority of God over every sphere of life—personal, social, political—and over every decision we make—in relationships, in career, in lifestyle— is to place a precious human life into those hands that are best able to shape and direct it for His glory and our good.

The alternative is surrender to the pressures, demands, and manipulations of others around us even while we continue to insist that we are under no authority and free from all control. In spite of our proud boast, we find over and over again that the petty tyranny of self has to give way to the stronger tyranny of others. We are saved from such a fate only by a willing surrender to the authority of "our Father in heaven." We are most free when most obedient, most our own when most His; we stand tall when we kneel before Him.

The fatherhood of God is no "of course" doctrine. It has implications. The implication of fatherhood is honor; the obligation of honor is obedience. This was the message of Old Testament prophets such as Malachi: "'A son honors his father, and a servant his master. If I am a father, where is the honor due me? If I am a master, where is the respect due me?' says the Lord Almighty" (Malachi 1:6).

It is impossible to give God honor without obedience. To sentimentalize this fatherhood and sanitize it of mastery is to offer insult, not adoration. Prophets like Isaiah poured scorn on those who reduced obedience to liturgy: "When you come to appear before me, who has asked this of you, this trampling of my courts? Stop bringing meaningless offerings! Your incense is detestable to me" (Isaiah 1:12–13).

The call to hallow the name of this Father is (as we shall see in another chapter) a call to action as well as adoration: "Stop doing wrong, learn to do right! Seek justice, encourage the oppressed. Defend the cause of the fatherless, plead the cause of the widow" (Isaiah 1:16–17). These are among the much-denied absolutes of life. But while we defend the existence of absolutes against the relativism that has marked much modern thought, we must realize that they are not self-existent qualities, isolated philosophical "givens." Rather they are predicated on the character of the God who is there for everyone at all times. They are personal qualities in God and authoritative demands from God before they are ethical absolutes in some abstract independent way.

Such obedience as God our Father requires of us, however, is of a very special and specific type: it is to be free, grateful, and above all loving. Love must be its motivation and more love its outcome; a love learned from Him before given to Him; a love in return for a love received.

When love fuels obedience, obedience goes far— and fast: "I run in the path of your commands," the psalmist writes, "for you have set my heart free" (Psalm 119:32). This love in turn flows from encountering and receiving the love of God our Father, a love that cost Him dearly: "For God so loved the world that he gave his one and only Son, that whoever believes in him shall not perish but have eternal life" (John 3:16).

The implications of that are brought out by the apostle John in his first epistle:

> Dear friends, since God so loved us, we also ought to love one another. . . . God is love. Whoever lives in love lives in God, and God in him. . . . Love is made complete among us so that we will have confidence on the day of judgment, because in this world we are like him. (1 John 4:11, 16–17)

NOTE

1. Harry Blamires, *Where Do We Stand?* (London: SPCK, 1980), 73.

Chapter Nine

A FATHER
WHO DISCIPLINES

*O*ften we do not like discipline, its controls or its directions, and sometimes we actively, even passionately, resent it. In extreme cases there are children who leave home because of such disputes with parental authority and discipline, and more who would like to! More often there are teenagers and adults whose lives are in a mess because they did not have the loving, firm discipline that children need and parents should give. Children need discipline, and discipline demands effort—on both sides. The parent who cares will make that effort. God is the model here too.

The father who cares is also a father who disciplines. God has no "spoiled children" as we use the term. From very early times His wisdom warned indulgent parents: "Folly is bound up in the heart of a child, but the rod of discipline will drive it far from him" and marked such discipline as a necessary part of love: "He who spares the rod hates his son, but he who loves him is careful to discipline him" (Proverbs 22:15; 13:24).

Whatever our attitudes toward corporal punishment, this early principle given to us for the development of our children reflects an ingredient in God's method of developing His children, believers who are growing to maturity in character and faith. Like our children, we too are threatened by selfishness and rebelliousness; we too can become distracted by the toys of life from its responsibilities. Like them, we might never learn our lessons if our Father did not correct us and remind us, sometimes sharply, who we belong to and what standard is expected of us. The writer of Hebrews explains: "My son, do not make light of the Lord's discipline, and do not lose heart when he rebukes you, because the Lord disciplines those he loves, and he punishes everyone he accepts as a son" (12: 5–6).

The writer of Hebrews is writing to a community of Jewish believers who are suffering persecution at the hands of their fellow countrymen. Their early zeal and courage are diminishing. They are warned to pay "more careful attention" to the gospel they have heard, so that they do not "drift away" (2:1). Later he reminds them of the meaning of God's loving discipline: "You have forgotten that word of encouragement that addresses you as sons: 'My son, do not make light of the Lord's discipline, and do not lose heart when he rebukes you, because the Lord disciplines those he loves, and he punishes everyone he accepts as a son.' Endure hardship as discipline; God is treating you as sons" (12:5–7).

When surrounding pressures try to force us into silence or to persuade us into compromise, we find within ourselves fears and selfishness and disloyalties that need the rebuke of our Father as well as the encouragement to stand firm, to speak out, to hold fast to what is right and true. That is what we have here.

To say the "Our Father" in private may give us comfort, but to serve our Father in public may well lead us to heaven through painful places. In a world that has many gods or a god other than the God and Father of our Lord Jesus Christ, we too may have to "endure hardship" and the discipline of true children. But it is precisely *there,* in the "avoidable sufferings" that meet Christian faith and obedience in this world, that we "submit to the Father of our spirits" (12:9).

Has God "disciplined" you? Are you suffering "because of righteousness"(Matthew 5:10)? Have you resented it, feared it, fought it? Did you think He *owed you* a favor? Have you learned the lesson now? Have you *submitted* to the Father? That is the decisive thing. In our suffering and setbacks, we may initially feel resentment, but we will soon realize that the Father owes us nothing but Himself—and He will never deny us that.

God's disciplines are only meant to draw us closer to Himself. They do not signify rejection but its opposite. We can comfort ourselves with this and act upon it. What parent meeting a trusting hand and a tearful face, rebellion in full surrender, independence seeking reconciliation, shame seeking solace, has not drawn closer than ever the child he or she loved—and disciplined.

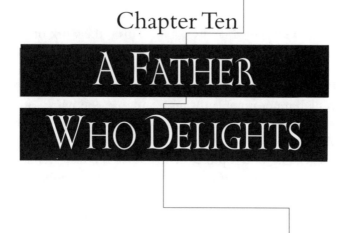

Chapter Ten

A FATHER WHO DELIGHTS

*P*arents should not only have real affection for their children but show it too. It is always sad to meet parents who cannot say or show their feelings directly (often because *their* parents could not). God our Father can help us break the legacy of previous generations, and as Christ is more perfectly formed in us we should become more integrated and more able to express our feelings.

For some of us it is easy to show our feelings. In my home hugs are almost compulsory, and although our own sons are now strapping six-foot men I still insist on the occasional hugging session. Every child should know that a father does not only correct, he also cuddles, and there are times when we too feel the embrace of God warming our hearts and strengthening our spirits. It may be in solitary prayer or in a crowded celebration; it may be at a time of great distress or one of great joy; it may be as we read the Book that was written for us or admire the beauty of creation, which is God's other book in which we read His power and wisdom. This is the work of the Spirit.

The Holy Spirit is God-next-to-us; it is He, the Third Person of the holy and blessed Trinity, who lives in us with immeasurable patience and care, and who works with us seeking to shape us into the likeness of Christ. Much of this work is done by Him indirectly through our reading of Scripture, by means of the teaching and fellowship of the church, in personal prayer and in our resolve to act and react as Christ would have us do.

But there are also times when, through the direct witness of the Holy Spirit, God communicates to us something of His love, His joy, His purity, and His peace. Paul writes of such times: "For you did not receive a spirit that makes you a slave again to fear, but you received the Spirit of sonship. And by him we cry 'Abba, Father.' The Spirit himself testifies with our spirit that we are God's children" (Romans 8:15–16).

We see examples of this happening with great dramatic force in the book of Acts: to the disciples on the day of Pentecost in Acts 2; to the half-Jewish Samaritans in Acts 8; to the Gentile Cornelius and his household in Acts 10; and to a group of John the Baptist's converts caught in a time warp in Acts 19. In other words, wherever the gospel about Jesus went this privilege went with it. And church history abounds with examples that contradict attempts to restrict such direct, immediate experience of God to the New Testament times.

The New England theologian Jonathan Edwards combined one of the greatest minds of his time with the heart of a pastor, evangelist, and leader in the great eighteenth-century revival. Edwards recorded one of many such experiences which he had, while in meditation and prayer:

> Once as I rode out into the woods for my health in 1737, having alighted from my horse in a retired place, as my manner commonly has been, to walk for divine contemplation and prayer, I had a view that for me was extraordinary, of the glory of the Son of God as Mediator between God and man, and His wonderful, great, pure, and sweet grace and love, and meek and gentle condescension. This grace that appeared so calm and sweet appeared also great among the heavens. The Person of Christ appeared ineffably excellent, with an excellency great enough to swallow up all thought and conception, which continued, as near as I can judge, about an hour, which kept me the greater part of the time in a flood of tears and weeping aloud. I felt an ardency of soul to be, what I know not otherwise how to express, emptied and annihilated; to lie in the dust and to be full of Christ alone; to love him with a holy and pure love; to trust in him, to live upon him, to serve and follow him and to be perfectly sanctified and made pure with a divine and heavenly purity.[1]

Many others of that time and since have recorded such experiences of God's closeness and love. "Love fell in showers on my soul," recorded Welsh revival leader Howell Harris; "I felt my heart strangely warmed" testified the very rational John Wesley; "God revealed himself to me, and I had such an experience of His love that I had to ask him to stay His hand" wrote the nineteenth-century evangelist D. L. Moody years after his experience. An older contemporary of Moody, Charles Finney, records his own experience: "The Holy Spirit descended upon me in a manner that seemed to go through me, body and soul. No words can express the wonderful love that was shed abroad in my heart. I wept aloud with joy and love ."[2]

Church history is full of such testimonies. It is sadly true, however, that such experiences are all too rare for most of us, even in much lower degree. God's dealings with us in this world are still to a degree conditioned by its fallen state, and we do not see or feel Him as we would wish. Yet if such experiences are possible on earth, how glorious will be His intimacies in heaven!

NOTES

1. As quoted in D. Martyn Lloyd-Jones, *Joy Unspeakable* (Eastbourne, England: Kingsway, 1984), 79–80.
2. Charles Finney, *Charles G. Finney: An Autobiography* (London: The Salvation Army, n.d.), 17–18.

Chapter Eleven

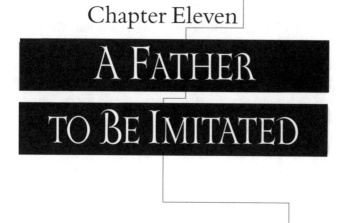

A FATHER
TO BE IMITATED

A holy God calls for a holy people; He may expect to see His family likeness in all His children. As He said long ago to His people Israel, "Be holy, because I am holy" (Leviticus 11:44,45), so He says now to the whole Israel of God, Jew and Gentile believers, ourselves included: "As obedient children, do not conform to the evil desires you had when you lived in ignorance. But just as he who called you is holy, so be holy in all you do; for it is written:'Be holy, because I am holy'" (1 Peter 1:14–15).

This is the foundation of Christian ethics. We hear absolutes denied and affirmed around us; but even for the Christian, ethical absolutes are not things that exist apart from God, floating free in the universe like elusive particles. It is God's holy character, His goodness and truth, His purity and wisdom that are the source and test of all that is good. When Moses, that servant of God, begged his master, "Now show me your glory," the reply of Yahweh was, "I will cause all my goodness to pass in front of

you" (Exodus 33:18–19). During the event, God pro-
claimed His "name," that is, His nature. He did so in
terms of a moral and spiritual relationship and its
demands and penalties: "The Lord, the Lord, the compassionate and gracious God, slow to anger, abounding in
love and faithfulness, maintaining love to thousands and
forgiving wickedness, rebellion and sin. Yet he does not
leave the guilty unpunished" (34:6–7).

All the human virtues of justice and mercy, love and
faithfulness, have their rise, not in the social convenience
of human society, but, before that, in the being of God
and thence in the constitution and consciences of men
and women made in His image.

Jesus taught His followers that for them these standards were not impracticable ideals but substantial possibilities. While others retained and reflected something of
God's moral judgments and characteristics because they
were His creation, believers could reach and practice a
higher perfection because they were His children. "Love
your enemies," Jesus said, "and pray for those who perse-
cute you, that you may be [i.e., consistently] sons of your
Father in heaven. . . . If you love those who love you . . .
Do not even pagans do that? Be perfect, therefore, as
your heavenly Father is perfect" (Matthew 5: 44–48).

Jesus Himself is the perfect model of that but gives
His followers power, too, to put into life what others put
into poetry: *to live out* human ideals and divine commands by *living in Him* in obedience and fruitfulness. "I
am the vine; you are the branches," He declared to His
followers. "If a man remains in me and I in him, he will
bear much fruit. . . . You are my friends if you do what I
command. . . . I have called you friends, for everything

that I learned from my Father I have made known to you" (John 15:5, 14–15).

Paul uses a strikingly familiar word when he writes to the Ephesian Christians: "Be imitators of God, therefore, as dearly loved children and live a life of love, just as Christ loved us and gave himself up for us as a fragrant offering and sacrifice to God" (Ephesians 5:1–2). His word "imitators" is the word from which we get the English word *mimics;* yet it is no mere mimicry that the apostle calls us to, but the cultivation of family traits and the practice of family ways "as dearly loved children." And, as everywhere, Christ is the model, and the mainspring of this is His perfect life and reconciling death. We belong to God because of Him, we are related to Him as to an elder brother (see John 20:17), and the great and final work of God is to conform us "to the likeness of his Son, that he might be the firstborn among many brothers" (Romans 8:29).

The imitation of God does not lie only in the cultivation of inner qualities but also in our public interaction with others. As the apostle Paul teaches the Ephesian Christians, it involves love in real life situations, resistance of life's seductions, the contradiction of surrounding darkness, and the challenge of what is with what can be (Ephesians 5:3–14). It is an imitation that comes into its own in situations of loving commitment such as marriage and family loyalty (Ephesians 5:22–6:4), and in situations of trust and responsibility (Ephesians 6:5–9). Remember the words of John: "God is love. Whoever lives in love lives in God, and God in him. In this way, love is made complete among us so that we will have confidence on the day of judgment because in this world we are like him" (1 John 4:16–17).

Chapter Twelve

WORSHIP

AS ADORATION

*I*n the first petition in the Lord's Prayer, Jesus sets forth the chief priority of all prayer: "Our Father in Heaven, *hallowed be your name.*" The glory of God is the supreme purpose and ultimate goal of every prayer.

To "hallow" means to treat as holy. It denotes reverence and suggests worship. God's name in biblical language stands for His nature, with its qualities and powers. To hallow God's name therefore is to hold Him in reverence, to worship and obey Him. It is to respond to what He has revealed of Himself, in appropriate ways; it is to adore His person, to respect His judgments, and to follow His ways. To pray "hallowed be your name" is to begin the process of worship.

What is worship? Our word comes from the Anglo-Saxon *worth-ship,* which means ascribing worth to God. He is worthy of all honor and praise, attention and obedience; and worship includes all of these. One of the finest and most well-known definitions of worship is that given by a late Archbishop of Canterbury, William Temple:

> Worship is the submission of all our nature to God. It is the quickening of the conscience by His holiness; the nourishment of the mind with His truth; the purifying of the imagination by His beauty; the opening of the heart to His love; the surrender of the will to His purpose—and all this gathered up in adoration, the most selfless emotion of which our nature is capable and therefore the chief remedy for that self-centredness which is original sin and the source of all actual sin.[1]

There are two parts to worship that make it what it is. Both are necessary to the very *being* of true worship. They are adoration and action.

We have known too little of adoration in recent times. Our secular-humanist Western society has long put man in the place of God. But our idols are letting us down. We are beginning to see that it is not only their feet that are made of clay. David Walsh writes:

> A shift of far-reaching significance is presently taking place within Western civilisation. . . . No longer can we naively subscribe to the fundamental conceit from which modernity began: that human beings are capable of providing their own moral and political order. . . . That experiment has run its course. Having been brought to its limits in the twentieth century, its bankruptcy has become fully exposed . . . human beings have again begun to look toward the source of order that lies beyond the self. A remarkable opening of the soul is taking place as we increasingly come to realise that we are not the self-sufficient ground of our own existence.[2]

The tragedy is that we now see many in this post-modern generation turning from new idols to old ones, from scientisms to superstitions; turning to New Age religion with its hybrid mix of ideas from Hinduism, Buddhism, and Western occultism, with its fads of astrology, reincarnation, "life-forces," and mystical experiences. Here all is one, all is God, and we are God. But how lonely and desolate it leaves so many: as disillusioned as ever with the gods they invent.

Nevertheless a power above all created power—real or imagined—does call to men and women: a power personal and good, holy and true; the God "who waits to be gracious." Unlike all idols, God inspires us to adore Him in silent contemplation and in joyful song because of His greatness and goodness, His majesty and grace, His power and love. And He does not call for adoration as a bribe, nor only as His due, but as something which is both His right and our fulfillment. We only find ourselves when we find the one true God. Our freedom lies in renouncing our independence and acknowledging His authority and rule. Only as we hallow His name do we remember our own:

Immortal, invisible, God only wise,
In light inaccessible hid from our eyes,
Most blessed, most glorious, the Ancient of Days,
Almighty, victorious, Thy great name we praise.[3]

One of the most profoundly moving discoveries for me was the knowledge that I can actually give God my Father pleasure in worship: that He can say to me as the lover says to the beloved in the Song of Songs: "Show me your face, let me hear your voice; for your voice is sweet, and your face is lovely" (Song of Songs 2:14). It seems so surprising, knowing the poverty of all I have to offer Him. But it is true for me and for all of us in His family. No fond parent ever sought out more their own child in a school choir or pageant than your divine and best parent seeks you out today and calls you to sing, to pray, to listen, and to respond in love and obedience. You may consider yourself to be just one of the crowd but to your Maker, Redeemer, and Friend you are quite irreplaceable. In F. W. Faber's words,

> Yet I may love Thee, too, O Lord,
> Almighty as Thou art,
> For Thou hast stooped to ask of me
> The love of my poor heart. [4]

The great spur to this in our church services must be, of course, the fact and the knowledge of the presence of God our Father in the midst of His people. We come to church to meet God—nothing less than that. And out of that meeting comes His glory and His praise on earth and our awe and adoration of Him, our hope and our joy. As Siegfried Grossman writes: "Every genuine religious experience is in essence an experience of the *presence* of God . . . of contact in the here and now with the overwhelming, joy-bringing, terrifying, saving and judging power of the transcendent."[5]

We must have adoration in our Christian service and experience. There must be times when God so fills the horizon that for a time other things fall back and fade and we can contemplate God alone: marveling at the mystery of His being and love, listening to His wisdom as He speaks in uncluttered moments, renewing our vows, and laying our lives gratefully and unresistingly in His hands.

A sight of God is a breathtaking thing. It can come in silence or in song, in reading, prayer, or sermon: a sight of God in His infinite perfection: "Infinite, eternal and unchangeable in His being, wisdom, power, holiness, justice, goodness and truth."[6]

But there is no sight of God to equal a sight of God in Christ, His Son and image. Ours is a Trinitarian faith and our worship must have its Trinitarian dimensions. Among men and angels there was no one who could say, "Anyone who has seen me has seen the Father" or insist that all must "honor the Son just as they honor the Father" (John 14:9; 5:23). In the sinless Son we see the holy Father, and in the Son's self-giving on the cross we see as nowhere else the integrity of the Father's righteousness and the extent of the Father's love. At His cradle, at His cross, and at His empty tomb, as well as now in the glory of His Father, the call is given to us all: "O come, let us adore Him, Christ the Lord."

The place of the Holy Spirit in all this is no less crucial. Without His illumination, our minds are dark with ignorance and prejudice; without His convicting and softening power, our hearts are proud and hard; without His fellowship channeling to us grace from the Son and love from the Father, our lives remain unchanged and our hearts empty of God. But by the Spirit, God comes in to fill us with the sense of God around us. It is the Spirit who takes us to worship, who opens us up to God, and who keeps these times of grace effective in our memories and daily lives. It is because of this ministry that St. Bernard of Clairvaux (1090–1153) could say: "I never come to thee but by thee: I never go from thee without thee."

NOTES

1. William Temple (1881–1944), *Readings in St. John's Gospel,* as quoted in Robert Paterson, *The Monarch Book of Christian Wisdom* (Crowborough, England: Monarch, 1997), 282.
2. David Walsh, *After Ideology* (San Francisco: Harper & Row, 1990), 1.
3. Walter Chalmers Smith (1824–1908), "Immortal, Invisible, God Only Wise." In public domain.
4. F. W. Faber (1814–63), "My God, How Wonderful Thou Art." In public domain.
5. Siegfried Grossman (quoting Ernst Benz) in *Stewards of God's Grace,* trans. M. Freeman (Exeter, England: Paternoster, 1977), 64.
6. The Westminster Shorter Catechism, 1648, Question 4, "What Is God?"

Chapter Thirteen

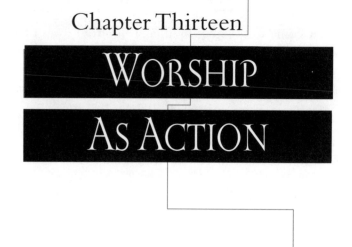

WORSHIP

AS ACTION

$\mathcal{A}$doration without action is in biblical faith unthinkable and incomprehensible. Worship, which is true and acceptable, involves the whole of a person (not just the mind or "soul") and the whole of life (not just the supposedly sacred time or space of special days and special places). "There is no space in which worship should not take place, no time when it should not occur, and no activity in which it should not happen," writes Miroslav Volf, the Croatian theologian.[1] True Christian worship is "worldly" and physical as well as "churchly" and spiritual. That is, it involves life in the body and in the world. Thus Paul writes, "I urge you, brothers, in view of God's mercy, to offer your bodies as living sacrifices, holy and pleasing to God—this is your spiritual act of worship" (Romans 12:1).

It is true that we need special times when we can stand apart from the pressures and distractions of life and when we can enter the experience of worshiping with others of the Christian community in order to be built up in faith and prepared for good works. But the out-working of what we learn and receive in the church meetings in the week before us and the world around us is *integral to* as well as crucial for true spiritual worship.

I am a preacher in Nottingham, England, and a few years ago a good friend of mine, the Reverend Dr. R. T. Kendall, asked me to speak in Westminster Chapel at his lunchtime service for people who work in that area of London. My short address to those business men and women contained much of what I want to emphasize here, and I believe the message will be plain and perhaps more forceful in its original form. So here is the talk, entitled "The Altar and the Office Desk":

Let me begin at the end. What I want to show is not merely that there is a connection between the desk and the altar, but that from Monday to Friday the desk is the altar.

I meet too many Christians who are fired up on Sunday and deflated by Wednesday because they feel their job is somehow second best in the Christian life. Sometimes they talk wistfully of going into something called "full-time Christian service," never thinking that what they are already doing is full-time Christian service because they are full-time Christian servants. Mark you, what they are presently engaged in may be *poor* full-time Christian service but probably only because they are poor full-time Christian servants—sloppy or selective or crotchety or unprincipled!

The idea that one vocation is more holy than anoth-er is pre-Reformation. The continental Reformers and

English Puritans of the sixteenth and seventeenth centuries baptized every occupation as a divine calling, an ordained and strategic employment in which God could be glorified. So should we all.

Eager young professionals, however, often feel they cannot give God the preeminence He deserves or serve His kingdom in the jobs they do. They could be door-to-door evangelizing among the shabby high-rise buildings downtown, but they have been confined to the prestigious office blocks of Westminster. They could be hacking their way through the jungle of the Amazon or the forests of Zaire (pith helmets provided) instead of taking the 7:00 A.M. commuter train from the south coast. Christian magnificence, they are sure, consists of wasting away in Nepal, not growing fat on luncheon vouchers in London's West End.

But wait a minute; if God has called you to London's business world, what business have you in Nepal? And if you are already on your way, how soon will you be back to continue in the Lord's work? To come a little nearer home, I have seen successful men enter the pastoral ministry who were never successful there or thereafter. They dreamed a dream and forgot to wake up; they got a call and lost their calling. It was such a pity, such a waste. Better to be a better banker than a boring preacher; better to fill an export order than to empty a church.

It has always been a masterly piece of strategy on Satan's part to convince Christian people that the nearer you live to God, the more you withdraw from the world. This leaves his own territory unchallenged and unthreatened. Christian faith and spirituality is relegated to the harmless play area of private life. Even the conscientious

9-to-5 man can find himself living in two worlds: that of the office and that of the altar. Solid as a rock, steady as a well-rooted tree in his local church, he may well encounter little buffeting from Satan because he poses little threat to Satan's kingdom—at least he is unlikely to do much damage in the place where he can do most damage, which is not in the local neighborhood where he lives but in the multinational business where he works. Our greatest need is not for more Christians, not even for more Christians in the "right" places—we have plenty there as well as elsewhere—the greatest need is for Christians to be *what* they are *where* they are: perceptively, patiently, determinedly, even fiercely.

Revolutionaries are no threat segregated from the society they want to change. A desert island is the perfect place for them! And Christians are no great threat to Satan's kingdom and no great use to Christ's when huddled in house groups back home or massed in celebrations and festivals. Their Christian standards of justice, righteousness, and truth must challenge assumptions and redirect policies in their city life and business. Moonlighting for God in the twilight world of weekends at the local church is no substitute for "full-time Christian service" in the finance company or the insurance broker's. If your "real self" does not live in the real world, then it's in for an identity crisis. For which really is the true "you": you at the prayer meeting or you at the office; you with the Bible or you with the bank statements; you in theology or you in commerce? Have you become a commuter between the world and the kingdom of God?

The explosion comes when the kingdom of God *enters* the world, challenges Satan in his stronghold, and plots his downfall and the eradication of structures of evil: inequity, oppression, or discrimination.

It may be a surprise to some of us to learn that in the New Testament "worship" is associated more with what we do *after* the church meetings than in them! In Romans 12 what Paul describes as "your spiritual [or reasonable, even logical] act of worship" is not the performance of a liturgy or the enjoyment of fellowship and good preaching but the dedication to God of our *bodily* existence in the day-to-day world. It is as we make the office desk the altar, the factory floor our consecrated ground, our own self-giving to the world (not simply the church) our aim, that we most truly "offer our bodies as living sacrifices holy and pleasing to God."

This perspective does not make "going to church" redundant; it only makes it preparatory. It is not an end in itself but a means to an end; a ministry of encouragement that builds up the body of Christ on earth to speak and live for Him. The chief end of man is to glorify God—not in a vacuum, not in the abstract, but in the world of concrete realities, which is God's world and which needs most of all the concrete realities of the good news of Christ Jesus.

"When does the service begin?" whispered a visitor to someone sitting beside him in a Quaker meeting. "Just after the meeting ends!" was the reply.

NOTE

1. Miroslav Volf, "Worship As Adoration and Action in Worship" in *Adoration and Action,* ed. D. A. Carson (Carlisle, England: Paternoster, 1993), 204.

Chapter Fourteen

YOUR NAME
IS MY ADDRESS

When our prayers begin with God's glory, as Jesus' prayer did, they lead us from the preoccupation with ourselves that prevailed during out pre–conversion lives. However, that process of leaving ourselves behind takes time. It's not easy to reverse the habit of years when we lived not for God but for ourselves and forgot about our Maker who was also rightly our master. Our aim was happiness not holiness; but the further we went from holiness, the further we went from happiness too! The more we centered on self, the bigger grew the hole in the middle of our life.

Selwyn Hughes has said: "In all the years I have worked as a minister and a Christian counsellor I have never met a happy self-centred person. The self-centred are the unhappy and the frustrated. They express them-selves but then they don't like the self they express."[1]

In our own times we have raised self-centeredness from a list of the vices to a list of the virtues. Psychologist and Christian Paul Vitz protests against the glorification of the self-evident in much Western culture and life today:

> The relentless and single-minded search for and glorification of the self is at direct cross-purposes with the Christian injunction to *lose* the self. Certainly Jesus Christ neither lived nor advocated a life that would qualify by today's standards as "self-actualised." For the Christian self is the problem, not the potential paradise. Understanding this problem involves an awareness of sin, especially of the sin of pride; correcting this condition requires the practice of such unself-actualised states as contrition and penitence, humility, obedience and trust in God.[2]

It is when we begin to look away from ourselves to God to transfer our ultimate loyalty from us to Him, to say "Hallowed be *your* name" that our own healing and true self-fulfillment begin. It is part of the upside-down world of God's kingdom that as we lose ourselves in this way we find ourselves. Jesus said, "If anyone would come after me, he must deny himself and take up his cross daily and follow me. For whoever wants to save his life will lose it, but whoever loses his life for me will save it" (Luke 9:23–24).

To deny oneself is not merely to give up things, whether sugar for Lent or smoking for good. To deny oneself is to deny the *centrality* of the self, which denies and disputes the centrality of God. Self-denial is not an unnatural self-hatred, for there is a natural and proper self-love. (Thus we are to love our neighbor as ourselves, as Jesus noted in Luke 10:27.) Nor does Christian self-denial require a masochistic or wasteful suppression of personality or gifts (which are God given and helpful to others). Our enemy is the glorification of self, the deification of self, and the tyranny of self over all who challenge its supremacy.

Such self-centeredness rivals God, and He opposes and seeks to destroy it. Self-centeredness is a corruption deep in the heart of the best of us and one that is exposed in its ugliness more and more as God comes near and lays claim on our lives. John Calvin, the great Swiss reformer, begins his famous *Institutes of the Christian Religion* with this statement: "Nearly all the wisdom we possess, that is to say true and sound wisdom, consists of two parts: the knowledge of God and of ourselves."[3] He goes on to show how these are crucially linked so that "it is certain that man never achieves clear knowledge of himself, unless he has first looked upon God's face, and then descends from contemplating him to scrutinize himself."[4] The significance of such self-knowledge, according to Calvin, is that "we always seem to ourselves righteous and upright and wise and holy—this pride is innate in all of us—unless by clear proof we stand convinced of our own unrighteousness, foulness, folly and impurity."[5]

The most dramatic biblical illustrations of this are Isaiah and Job. The young prophet Isaiah, confronted with the vision of God in the beauty of holiness, cries out, "Woe to me! . . . I am ruined! For I am a man of unclean lips, and I live among a people of unclean lips, and my eyes have seen the King, the Lord Almighty" (6:5). And Job responds similarly: "My ears had heard of you but now my eyes have seen you. Therefore I despise myself and repent in dust and ashes" (42:5).

We see, then, that the only true self-image comes from looking at God and not at ourselves. This is surely the most crucial of all factors in self-understanding and self-assessment. However, we ought not to stop with Isaiah or Job's initial experience. For the love of God raises those whom the holiness of God slays, and only pride stays in the dust.

God is like the father in the parable of the prodigal son (see Luke 15:11–32). His forgiveness is so complete that He brings us out of infamy into privilege, and gives us beauty for ashes. He turns despair into joy. In grace He not only forgives us, He changes us. He not only changes us, He adopts us. He gives us not merely a fresh start but a new identity and a new relationship; one that is unbreakable and which will challenge sin and backsliding, encourage godliness in all its forms, and enable us to say, "I have been crucified with Christ and I no longer live, but Christ lives in me. The life I live in the body, I live by faith in the Son of God, who loved me and gave himself for me" (Galatians 2:20). It is this spirit that in grateful adoration says, "Hallowed be your name."

When we find God we find ourselves, our real worth, our true home. True, there has to be a full confession and a genuine renunciation of sin; there has to be a sloughing off of the old attitudes of lifestyle. The father of the returning prodigal son called for the best robe, but first there would have been the burning of the old rags. The ring for the finger and the sandals for the feet were put on a washed body. The celebration was in the father's home, not in the far-off pigsty. It is not in "the distant country" far from God that we find out who we are, but in the Father's house and at the Father's feet and in the Father's arms. "Hallowed be *your* name."

NOTES

1. Selwyn Hughes, *The Christian Councellor's Pocket Guide* (Eastbourne, England: Kingsway, 1982), n. p.
2. Paul Vitz, *Psychology As Religion* (Tring, England: Lion, 1977), 81.
3. John Calvin, *Institutes [Instructions] of the Christian Religion,* vol. 1 (Philadelphia: Westminster, 1977), 35.
4. Ibid., 37.
5. Ibid..

PART TWO

"YOUR KINGDOM COME,
YOUR WILL BE DONE
ON EARTH AS IT IS IN HEAVEN"

Chapter Fifteen

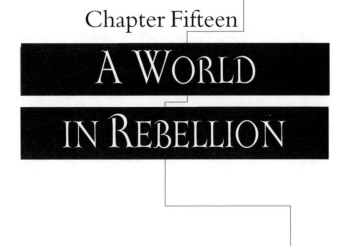

A WORLD

IN REBELLION

*E*very Valentine's Day my wife, Valerie, and I chuckle over some of the more colorful messages that appear in *The Times*. Silly names and soppy notes make for light relief amid the grim news. One message, though, was not to a lover from a lover but from grown-up children to their parents. In a touching tribute and a winsome confession, they wrote: "The rebels failed, for our Utopia was the home we fought to leave."

It seemed to me then, as now, that that is the most perfect description of our race and its world in its long history of rebellion and independence from its Creator and Lawgiver. We are a race of rebels doggedly determined to go it alone and to build our kingdoms; to pursue our own plans, in our own strength and according to our own rules. Jesus prayed, "Your kingdom come," and Christ's call for the kingdom of God was made then, as now, in a world system that does not recognize nor welcome the kingdom.

Almost from the beginning, men and women have determined to build their own kingdoms. The essence of Adam and Eve's sin as told in the book of Genesis was rebellion. Their Creator had given them both freedom and boundaries, lordship and limits. (See Genesis 1:28; 2:17.) Their rebellion involved an attempt to take their freedom beyond its boundaries, to extend the lordship they had been given until it rivaled that of God—who gave it (see Genesis 3:5). Pride and foolishness, selfishness and the lust for power all combined in the seminal sin that seeded the race and left us a bitter harvest in every age and generation.

That rebellion against God, which disputes His right to rule over us, is born with us and remains in each of us. It is the boast of the arrogant and the shame of the humble, the "strength" of the unbeliever and the weakness of the Christian.

What is true of the individual is writ large in our societies. Very often the New Testament writers, and especially John, speak about "the world" in contrast to the people or church of God, and warn believers of a deep alienation, a profound antipathy, and a dangerous conflict between the two:

> Do not love the world or anything in the world. If anyone loves the world, the love of the Father is not in him. For everything in the world—the cravings of sinful man, the lust of his eyes and the boasting of what he has and does—comes not from the Father but from the world. The world and its desires pass away, but the man who does the will of God lives forever. (1 John 2:15–17)

By his term "the world" John means society constructed so as to keep God out of its affairs, society in its determined and deliberate godlessness. This world includes human politics, economics, ethics, and a life-style determined from within and without reference to God's character and will. When John tells us not to love "anything in the world," he is using strong language, not with regard to our society's excellences and achievements, practical or aesthetic, but with regard to its priorities and motivations in which God is refused His place of sovereignty and judgment. Since the fall of the race, human societies rich and poor, sophisticated and igno-rant, ancient and modern, including our own, have shared in this conspiracy to keep God out of their affairs.

There have been many substitutes for this kingdom. They have all failed. The late Bristish commentator Malcolm Muggeridge in one of his books recalled his years as a young journalist, full of hope in the politics of the day. Then he went to Moscow in the early 1930s and came face-to-face with the terrible realities around him. He wrote:

> How marvellous the Russian revolution seemed when it happened! A little bearded man wearing a cap, Lenin, had taken over the vast empire of the Tsars on behalf of the workers and peasants. . . . The words of the *Magnificat* had been fulfilled, certainly, the mighty had been put down from their seats and the humble and meek exalted, and now I had to face the unpalatable fact that the humble and meek, thus exalted, had become mighty in their turn and fit to be put down.[1]

The enemy of all our politics is ourselves. Our ideol-ogy and social engineering can never, despite all our immense resources, get the weakness and wickedness out of our hearts. Only God can do that—and He does not do it to order! Most of us want the inconveniences of sin rather than sin itself to be dealt with, but it is only on bended knee that we enter the kingdom, in full confession and sincere faith, humbling self and exalting God. We must come in full surrender to His lordship and His love.

Consider the apostle Paul's devastating indictment of the Gentile world of his own day. Once again pride, sophistication, and arrogance had combined to keep the true God out of human affairs: "They exchanged the truth of God for a lie," and the result was social alienation, sexual deviation and personal disintegration (Romans 1: 25, see also 28–31). The strong and stately edifice of the Roman Empire was doomed from within long before outside forces caused it to crumble.

At the close of the New Testament canon this theme reaches its climax, as the apostle John predicts the growth of empires and civilizations that oppose God and the gospel of His Son. Only the second coming of Christ to judgment will bring the hostility to an end and establish God's reign on earth: "The kingdom of the world has become the kingdom of our Lord and of his Christ, and he will reign for ever and ever" (Revelation 11:15).

Meantime the people of God wait and work and witness in an environment hostile to their faith and first loyalty. As they witness this world's cruelties and hear its blasphemies and false philosophies, they may cry in one urgent longing: "Our Father in heaven, *Your kingdom come.*"

NOTE

1. Malcolm Muggeridge, *Tread Softly, for You Tread on My Jokes* (London: Fontana, 1968), 22–23.

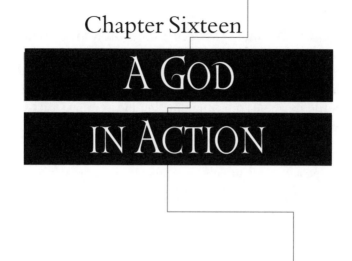

Chapter Sixteen

A GOD

IN ACTION

he kingdom of God, which we pray for in the Lord's Prayer, is a kingdom magnificent in its plan and scope. The kingdom plan and purpose are chronicled in the Holy Scriptures. For the Bible is the history of salvation, the history of God in action for the salvation of the human race. The book of Genesis recounts beginnings: the beginning of the universe, the beginning of our world, the beginning of humankind, the beginning of sin in our world—and the beginning of redemption. We learn that God's promise is as old as His curse (see Genesis 3:15) and that no sooner had the race made in His image rebelled and begun to disintegrate (4:8) than God began a process of rescue and reversal. He gathered to Himself a people who would "call on the name of the Lord" and live with righteousness and justice on the earth (4:25–6; 6:9). Through global judgment (the Flood) and international chaos (Babel and after) that process continued. At times God's purposes seemed about to fail. But "is anything too hard for the Lord?" (18:14).

The call of Abraham began the most important stage in Old Testament salvation history. It narrowed God's purposes down to a single people but only in order to broaden those purposes out to embrace all peoples:

> The Lord had said to Abram, "Leave your country, your people and your father's household and go to the land I will show you. I will make you into a great nation and I will bless you; I will make your name great, and you will be a blessing. I will bless those who bless you, and whoever curses you I will curse; and all peoples on earth will be blessed through you." (12:1–3)

The family of Abraham becomes the tribes of Israel, enslaved in Egypt but "redeemed" from bondage and led out by Moses in the great redemptive act of the Exodus. At Sinai the twelve tribes become the chosen nation, the people and bride of Yahweh; a nation "set apart"' (as the word *holy* basically means) for God. Moses leads them to the borders of their Promised Land but it is Joshua who leads them into it. In spite of the people's frequent tendency to forget their high calling and to compromise with the heathen nations around, God preserves Israel's identity by means of the Law given to Moses; He sternly reminds the nation of her unique calling through the prophets. In their lives and in their message the prophets embody the "faithful remnant" who stay true to the nation's life and calling.

However, their prophetic messages of exposure and judgment becomes to them "the burden of the Lord," which often weighs heavily upon their hearts, for they live in hard times. This burden is lightened only by the vision of a better time that lays in the future, when God will come to the world and to His people in final judgment and salvation to establish His own rule of righteousness and peace once and for all throughout the whole earth.

Isaiah most famously and most beautifully speaks of that time. He does so, for instance, in the Christmas readings of chapters 9 and 11, pointing to the child whose name will be called "Wonderful Counselor" and "Prince of Peace," whose government will never end, on whom the "Spirit of the Lord will rest" and who will judge the world with righteousness so that "the earth will be full of the knowledge of the Lord as the waters cover the sea" (Isaiah 9:6–7; 11:2, 9).

In that day nations long hostile to one another will be at peace, for the one true God will be their unity. (See 2:1–3; 19:19–25.) Israel will come into her own, and the nations will share her God and her glory in a new heaven and a new earth. (See Isaiah 51:1–2, 7; 60:1–3; 65:17.) This time of widespread judgment and world renewal is called in the Old Testament writings "The Day of the Lord"; and associated with it is the kingdom of God which that day ushers in.

As our Savior taught, we are to pray for this godly kingdom, which both now is and will find its final fulfillment in Christ's return to earth. "The kingdom of God in the Bible," wrote George Beasley-Murray, "primarily means God exercising His sovereign power in judgement and salvation."[1] The Dutch theologian Herman Ridderbos described it as "the kingly self-assertion of God in justice and in mercy."[2] In a phrase, it is the rule of God in the reign of grace. Notice that God's "kingdom" in all this is not an *area* over which He rules but an *activity* in which He extends His rule. Perhaps it would be better therefore to understand this part of the Lord's Prayer as "Your kingship come."

Most important, the Old Testament teaches that Yahweh comes *in person* to carry out His kingdom plan. The coming of the kingdom is unthinkable without the coming of the King. It is by divine intervention, not social evolution, that the age of peace and prosperity dawns. As I once heard it put, the kingdom is God "king-ing it" among us!

NOTES

1. George Beasley-Murray, *The Coming of God* (Exeter, England: Paternoster, 1983), 14.
2. Herman Ridderbos, *The Coming of the Kingdom* (Philadelphia: Presb. & Ref., 1976), 19.

Chapter Seventeen

THE COMING
OF THE KING

*W*hen Jesus appeared on the public scene proclaiming in Galilee and preaching in the synagogues, "The time is fulfilled, and the kingdom of God is at hand" (Mark 1:15 RSV), there was enormous interest and excitement. Jesus was proclaiming the beginning of God's long-promised intervention in human affairs, the promised restoration of all things, the final judgment and salvation of God. It is equally clear that from the start Jesus connected this kingdom with *Himself.* In the synagogue at Nazareth He said after reading the first two verses of Isaiah 61: "Today this scripture is fulfilled in your hearing."

"He went to Nazareth, where He had been brought up," Luke reports, and entered the synagogue on the Sabbath day as He normally did. Then:

> He stood up to read. The scroll of the prophet Isaiah was handed to him. Unrolling it, he found the place where it is written: "The Spirit of the Lord is on me, because he

has anointed me to preach good news to the poor. He has sent me to proclaim freedom for the prisoners and recovery of sight for the blind, to release the oppressed, to proclaim the year of the Lord's favor." (Luke 4:16–19)

Jesus was reading from one of the prophecies of universal restoration in Isaiah. In the politically charged atmosphere of early first-century Galilee, however, it would have been regarded as one of the revolutionary prophecies of the Old Testament. There the announcement "the kingdom of heaven is at hand" would have been heard by many as equivalent to "the revolution is about to begin!" Throughout His public ministry Jesus was alive to the popular expectation that the Messiah would lead Israel, God's chosen people, to throw off the Roman yoke.

In Nazareth Jesus created growing consternation and fury as He in fact modified the reading from Isaiah, *leaving out* some of the very things they wanted to be emphasized. He read of "the year of the Lord's favor," but not "the day of vengeance of our God"; He inserted an extra line from Isaiah 58:6, "freedom for the prisoners," but not what follows, "and break every yoke." As Joachim Jeremias and others have pointed out, the Greek of verse 22 could be translated very differently from our popular versions to read "All *protested* [the Greek verb is literally "all bore witness" and can mean to affirm or to witness against someone] with one voice and were *furious* [the Greek verb can mean amazed or horrified] because He spoke [only] about mercy."[1] He finally snapped the slender thread of patience in His hearers by referring to God's compassion for the Gentiles, sometimes even giving them priority over His own Jewish people. (See Luke 4:24–30.)

The listeners at Nazareth were both amazed and angered because Jesus had announced the revolution without vengeance on Israel's enemies. It was a revolution of mercy, peace, and blessing—to Jew and Gentile alike. This was not yet the Day of Judgment but "the year of the Lord's favor."

In the three years of His public ministry Jesus continued to preach the kingdom of God and to practice its presence in words, works, and wonders. (For example, see Luke 11:20; 17:20–21). "Jesus affirms [the kingdom's] presence in the world in and through his word and work," wrote George Beasley-Murray.[2]

The sovereign work of Yahweh, which was to defeat all evil and overcome all opposition and achieve a transformed earth, had been decisively inaugurated by Jesus in His powerful deeds and authoritative words. Hence, Jesus could speak interchangeably of "my father's kingdom" and "my kingdom." We read of "the kingdom of our Lord and of his Christ" (Revelation 11:15). Where God reigns, Christ Jesus His Son is King. But what king was ever like this? Many kingdoms have been built on the blood of their enemies, but here is a kingdom that will be built on the blood of its Founder and King; a kingdom won not by self-assertion but by self-surrender, a kingdom whose king is its universal servant (see Mark 10:45; John 13:3–7); in short, an upside-down kingdom that would challenge every assumption, search every conscience, and change every life it touched.

Theologian and author Richard Bauckham summed

up the significance and effect of Jesus' kingdom ministry particularly well:

> In relation to demonic oppression, conquest;
> in relation to misrepresentation of God's rule, sharp
>   rebuke;
> in relation to selfish complacency, warning;
> in relation to sin and failure, forgiveness and assurance
>   of love;
> in relation to sickness, healing;
> in relation to material need, provision of daily bread;
> in relation to exclusion, welcoming inclusion;
> in relation to desire for power, an example of humble
>   and loving service;
> in relation to death, life;
> in relation to false peace, painful division,
>   but in relation to enmity, reconciliation.[3]

Jesus saw the kingdom of God as both *present* in a provisional way, in His ministry of mighty works and preaching, and *future,* at the harvest of the world at the end of the age, when He as the Son of Man would come again in His glory to establish the reign of God in fullness throughout the earth. (See Matthew 11:5–6; 12:28; compare with Matthew 13:24–29; 25:31–46; Mark 14:62.) But in both its present and future forms, the kingdom was uniquely and crucially allied with Himself. As He warned His critics among the Pharisees, to look for the (coming of) the kingdom of God apart from Jesus was to mistake it and miss it (see Luke 17:20–21), for the kingdom of God was there and then, "among" them (17:21 NIV margin), in their midst. In Jesus, God had already come to inaugurate and work out His reign in grace. It was from the start, and would be until the final judgment, "the acceptable year of the Lord" (Luke 4:19 RSV).

Already men and women were pressing into it and suffering for it, Jesus said (see Matthew 11:12). He described the kingdom as a treasure within reach of all who heard its message (Matthew 13:44–46), but one which would be taken away from an unbelieving nation and given to the Gentiles (Matthew 21:43). In various parables He described it as a feast to which all were invited, a seed growing secretly, and a dragnet trawling the generations.

Its fullness, however, lies in the future. That future is today as ever the church's goal and her inheritance (Matthew 19:28–30; 2 Timothy 4:1).

The kingdom in its fullness lies in the future, and in the future not as a human evolution but as a divine consummation (Matthew 25:31–34). It is a future in God and with God (Colossians 3:1–3), and it lies nowhere else. The politics of earth cannot substitute for, or even achieve, the kingdom of heaven. "Utopia" is nowhere, but our life in the kingdom of God is "wrapped up with Christ in God" (my translation of Colossians 3:4) and is safe and sure. This future emphasis is needed lest we make claims which are unsubstantiable in the present "age." Here the kingdom has only come provisionally. Caesar, sin, and sickness still hold great sway but not to defeat the purposes of God. (See John 18:36; 19:10–11.) Here we too can claim much by faith, but because we live in the world of the Fall and share to some extent its fallenness still, we must reckon with Paul's words, "your body is dead because of sin, yet your spirit is alive because of righteousness" (Romans 8:10). This knowledge saves us from a foolish triumphalism such as the Corinthian believers fell into. (See 1 Corinthians 4:8–13; 2 Corinthians 12:7–10.)

The Christian and the church thus live "between the times": after the kingdom of God has come but before it has fully come. Our striking witness to the world has to be as a people who live the future in the present. Our church communities are to be outposts of that future world in this present world, communities of men and women who are struggling with all the realities of this life but who do so as children of the kingdom, journeying toward its glorious fullness. We go with that light flickering on our faces and praying always, "Your kingdom come."

NOTES

1. See David Bosch, *Transforming Mission* (Maryknoll, N. Y.: Orbis Books, 1991), 110–11; and I. H. Marshall, *The Gospel of Luke* (Exeter, England: Paternoster, 1978), 185–86.
2. George Beasley-Murray, *Jesus and the Kingdom of God* (Exeter, England: Paternoster, 1986), 227.
3. Richard Bauckham, *The Bible in Politics* (London: SPCK, 1989), 143.

Chapter Eighteen

THE COMMUNITY

OF THE KINGDOM

*J*esus not only preached the kingdom of God but established its community in relation to Himself. From the beginning He gathered disciples who were both part of this community and the means of its increase, and He taught them in ways that distinguished them from the world at large. Thus the Sermon on the Mount, for example, contains not a *prescription* for society in general but a *description* of the children of the kingdom: they are the poor in spirit, the meek, the merciful, the pure in heart, and so on; and Jesus gives a corresponding series of directions for their lives that can only flow from such people, including heart obedience, spiritual worship, trust, and fruitfulness. Such principles of conduct set out in the Sermon on the Mount are both impracticable and quite impossible without the love and power of God ruling the heart. That is why the Sermon can never be used as a blueprint for society at large in its secular state.

What Jesus is doing, here and elsewhere, is speaking more to the church than to the world: to God's kingdom rather than Caesar's. For the church is to be the community of the kingdom: belonging to its King, walking by its laws, living in its powers, and inheriting its future. Although the kingdom in its fullness and universality is still in the future, Christ has set that future irresistibly in motion in the here-and-now, bringing its life to us and into us.

The church is not the kingdom, but the church is the *product* of the kingdom and the *channel* of the kingdom: an outpost in history of what will one day succeed history as we now see it in a fallen world. The church is to be the sign of the future to the world: the sign of *God's* future. As church growth expert Eddie Gibbs puts it, "The Church is more than the herald announcing the message, it is a demonstration model which gives credence to the effectiveness of that message."[1] So the church is to exhibit the kingdom of God and the life of "the age to come" in a life of reconciliation and peace, truth and justice, love and faith. Its members are to touch the untouchables, include the excluded, outface the powers that keep people from God, and model the life of the kingdom in our church communities—the churches. These are to be communities of reconciled people in societies of alienated people; communities of caring people in a world of individuals too preoccupied to care; communities of love and peace, encouragement and strength, commitment and loyalty.

This is the life of the kingdom in the church of God. Such a life may at present be only partially and imperfectly grasped and lived, and it might appear weak and irrelevant to the world. But it was and is a mustard-seed beginning of a new and mighty future, a parable of what would be; leading us by small steps toward a great destiny —for the meek will inherit the earth at the coming of the King.

Jesus' message about the kingdom is essentially one of joy. He preached the good news of the kingdom, and the good news is that it is offered to "the poor": the sinful, the failed, the excluded, the hopeless. It is to those who receive it "like a little child" in the humility of faith (Luke 18:17) who discover its riches and its joy. It is the treasure hidden in a field, the pearl of great value, and those to whom it is offered are happy to pay any price for it. The joy of receiving it is a joy shared by God Himself: indeed it is *His* joy in us becoming one with our joy in Him. (See Luke 15:7, 10, 23–24.) The church of God is to be a community of joy and celebration.

Have you noticed how often in the Gospels we read about parties, banquets, feastings, and merriment? Jesus seems to have attended more parties than funerals and very often uses the image of a banquet in His parables.[2] There is, in fact, serious theology involved in this!

The Jews looked forward to the "messianic banquet" in the age to come, and Jesus used this imagery to express the joy of that age. Moreover His presence at celebrations private and public, usually with Him at the center, was a present, visible demonstration of that joy, indicating the critical truth that the long promised and awaited kingdom was even then present in Jesus' words and deeds. The most famous of His "party parables" is that of the great banquet where those originally invited to a feast excused themselves in various ways and were replaced by "the poor, the crippled, the blind and the lame" (Luke 14:16–24). The point, not to say the sting, is well made by E. Linneman:

> The Pharisees do not believe that the kingdom of God is beginning now and see no connection between this event and Jesus' table fellowship with the lost. But Jesus places the situation in the light of a parable in which some people are not prepared to respect the fact that *the meal has already begun* and have to put up with the consequences. Anyone who is not willing to be summoned to the first course does not get to taste the meal proper.[3]

The deep seriousness of this is graphically expressed in various parables and sayings: in the dismay of the foolish virgins locked out of the wedding feast, in the confusion and shame of those who have no "wedding garment" for the feast, and most starkly in the weeping, wailing, and gnashing of teeth of those unable to enter the kingdom because they have rejected the King, while others rejoice to be in it because, for all their sin, they accepted Him (see Matthew 24:1–14; 25:1–13).

When we pray, "Your kingdom come," we should realize that we are praying about something very serious: We are praying about something that will be as terrible to some as it will be joyful to others. We are praying for the closing of the door as well as opening of the gates; the final exclusion of the unbelieving, including the undecided, as well as the entrance of a redeemed and reconciled race into its destiny, the kingdom prepared for it from the foundation of the world (see Matthew 25:10, 34). We are praying for the end of the old order with its space for repentance as well as its pain and its tears. (See

Romans 2:5; 2 Peter 3:9; Revelation 21:4.) In its place, we are praying for the new heaven and new earth and for the final state of the city of God which will enfold nations but exclude the ungodly (see Revelation 21:1, 6–8, 22–27).

In summary, whenever we pray, "Your kingdom come," we are praying, "Come, Lord Jesus; come quickly, for salvation and judgment."

NOTES

1 Eddie Gibbs, *I Believe in Church Growth* (London: Hodder & Stoughton, 1985), 142.

2. The image of the banquet is found in all four gospel accounts. See Matthew 8:11; 11:19; 22:1–14; 25:10; Mark 2:15–16, 19–20; 6:42–44; 8:8–9; 14:25; Luke 8:12–14, 15–24; 14:8; 15:1–2, 22–24; 19:5–10; John 2:1–10; 12:2; 21:9–13.

3. As quoted in George Beasley-Murray, *Jesus and the Kingdom of God* (Exeter, England: Paternoster, 1986), 121.

Chapter Nineteen

THE KINGDOM OF HEAVEN AND THE POLITICS OF EARTH

*I*n his study of ethics in the Old Testament, Christopher J. H. Wright makes the following observation about God's deliverance of Israel from Pharaoh's Egypt:

> One outstanding feature of the redemption achieved at the Exodus was its comprehensiveness. In that one sequence of events God gave to Israel a four-fold freedom: *politically* from the tyranny of a foreign autocratic power; *socially* from the intolerable interference in their family life; *economically* from the burden of enforced slave-labour; *spiritually* from the realm of foreign gods into the unhindered worship of the Lord and covenant relationship with him.[1]

It is true that we do not live under the old covenant. Yet Wright's description reminds us of what God hates in the world and how His activity, in grace, works against the cruelties that disfigure human beings as well as societies. Consequently the work of God's kingdom should not be divorced from the world, and such activity will never be irrelevant to that society. However, neither should it be submerged in that society, lost in, or made redundant by different societies' social programs, developing ethics (where they do develop!), or democratic politics.

Here we encounter two extremes that the church has witnessed among "the children of the kingdom": withdrawal from the world and identification with the world; the abandonment of the state and surrender to the state; the failure to observe civil duty on the one hand and the failure to preserve Christian identity on the other hand.

When Jesus prayed for His church, He asked God for protection but not isolation: "My prayer is not that you take them out of the world but that you protect them from the evil one" (John 17:15). When Jesus said to Pilate, "My kingdom is not of this world . . . my kingdom is from another place" (John 18:36), He certainly did not mean that His kingdom had nothing to do with this world. He meant His kingdom was not constructed from the materials of this world—its politics, its powers, its historical processes. It is of God and from God and comes from another world. However, it does come *into* this world (into what we in our vanity call "the real world") and affects its people and its politics, its social order and its reforms.

As the children of the kingdom, the people of God are said by Jesus to be "the salt of the earth" and "the light of the world" (Matthew 5:13, 14). Both of these imply contact with our societies and both suggest that something is very wrong in those societies, needing our message and its demonstration. Salt, after all, was used as a preservative on dead carcasses, not live animals, and the force of Jesus' metaphor suggests the spiritual death and tendency to decay that inevitably characterizes society apart from God. There is a law of entropy, a tendency to break down, in fallen human nature and its organizations and institutions. The innate selfishness of the human heart and its capacity for cruel exploitation threaten all its institutions: marriages, work relations, social services, good citizenship (think just of your tax returns!), political and international affairs. Only the universal grace of God preserves human society from its own evil, and God has ordained the people of His kingdom to show and to urge a better way.

However, we live in a world that has long rejected the kingship of God and frequently scorns the voice of His people. Human societies have set up a series of substitutes for His kingdom, culminating in the modern, secular state and its liberal democracy. We may well believe that in the democratic state the politics of this world have reached the peak of their evolution. But its problems have continued to multiply and its failures are clearly seen in our modern history and in our daily newspapers. The twentieth century saw the utter failure of Victorian optimism. The expected golden age produced not Tennyson's "parliament of man" but Stalin's gulags and Hitler's death camps, war casualties in scores of millions, and a cold war between two superpowers with unimaginable potential for destruction.

Today, with world wars behind us and nuclear war less likely, we are witnessing once more the rise of old nationalisms and tribalisms, distorted and poisoned by centuries-long hatreds. A multiplicity of small powers, as virulent and cruel as any superpower could ever be, is filling the political and military vacuums with human greed, prejudice, and violence. As I write, twenty-five wars are taking place in various parts of the globe, creating huge suffering, and all the politics of man and the diplomacy of nations cannot bring peace to our world.

Even where there is no civil strife, there is betrayal and breakdown in marriages; exploitation, injustice, and alienation in the marketplace; and growing crime and violence in our cities.

In the midst of this, the kingdom of God is persistently at work, especially in and through the lives and witness of Christian men and women who are truly living by the principles of the kingdom and not the prejudices and preoccupations of the world. These are to be identified with the world yet separate from it—identified with its needs and its problems but separate from its conspiracy to keep God out of its solutions! Hence, at one and the same time, we are the world's friends and its critics, we challenge as well as comfort, demolish as well as construct. (See 2 Corinthians 10:4–5.)

We must make the best of what is and work for what is not, and at the end of the day still cry, "This is not enough!" We are to be occupied in this world but not preoccupied with it nor with our successes in it, short of the rescue of men and women to eternal salvation, "for the form of this world is passing away" (1 Corinthians 7:29–31 NASB). Hence the waiting church, though she is always to be working as well as waiting, will still pray as she works for a better world: "Your kingdom come."

NOTE

1. Christopher J.H. Wright, *Living As the People of God* (Leicester, England: InterVarsity, 1985), 74; my italics.

Chapter Twenty

THE KINGDOM OF GOD

AND THE MISSION

OF THE CHURCH

A call to world mission is at the heart of Christianity. Even before the coming of Christ, it was central to God's plan and to the prophetic vision of the Old Testament (see Genesis 12:3; Isaiah 2:1–5). God is a missionary God, the Bible is a missionary book, and Jesus called for a missionary church. He said He was the light, not only of Israel but of the world, the Good Shepherd who had sheep far beyond that "sheep pen." He said He was the one who would drive out "the prince of this world" and "draw all men" to Himself (John 12:31–32). And His unique claims laid upon His followers a call to make Him known to the world for which He died.

From the start Jesus placed world mission near the top of the church's agenda. At the start of His public ministry, His call to Simon and Andrew, who were fishing in the Sea of Galilee, was, "Come, follow me, and I will make you fishers of men" (Mark 1:17). Before ascending to heaven, He repeated the same call as a commission, and indeed a command: "All authority in heaven and on earth has been given to me. Therefore go and make disciples of all nations, baptizing them in the name of the Father and of the Son and of the Holy Spirit" (Matthew 28:18–19).

This note is sounded similarly at the end of the other Gospels (Mark 16:15; Luke 24:47; John 20:21), and Acts is to an extent the record of the apostolic obedience to it. The mission of the early church and its leaders issued not only from a Christ-given command but also from a Pentecostal experience of joy and power in the Holy Spirit. The whole church was involved in this expansion; it was spontaneous, natural, and quite unstoppable. Leaders like Paul and Peter planted churches in the Middle East, Turkey, and Europe; but they also congratulated the young churches on their public and well-known witness. (See, for example, 1 Thessalonians 1:7–10.) The New Testament church was self consciously an evangelizing church and a missionary church.

No one then could have foreseen twenty centuries of continuing world history with its space for repentance (see 2 Peter 3:9), the advances and setbacks of church history, or a present-day Christian church numbering believers in hundreds of millions. However, their astonished delight at our numbers would surely have been tempered in many places by dismay at our loss of vision, our worldliness, and our sheer anonymity in the world.

In so many of our comfortable, affluent Western churches, world mission has indeed been the church's withered arm. There has been a failure to realize the plight of the lost and the potential of the saved. Our comparatively secure, trouble-free existence has led us into counting many blessings but not missed opportunities. Our building programs far outstrip our mission strategies and our building funds dwarf our missionary giving. Many churches that support a missionary society never think of seriously praying that one of their own number may be sent, or of urging them to consider going with their church's full financial support and blessing. Yet few experiences more joyfully enlarge a church's vision and give them a taste of the Acts vision.

Most of us are embarrassed to witness openly; we would not dream of leaving promising careers and home comforts to take the message of Jesus to other nations and tribes. We even feel we have no right any longer to say or even think that people of other religions need to know the Gospel of Jesus to be saved. But if Jesus is right, they do! His apostles too lived in a pluralistic and religiously tolerant society, but they challenged its gods and changed the course of history with the spread of their proclamation of the truth that is in Jesus. Michael Green has renewed that challenge in these words:

> How can all religions lead to God when they are so different? . . . Christianity teaches that God both forgives a man and gives him supernatural aid. In Buddhism there is no forgiveness and no supernatural aid. The goal of all existence in Buddhism is *nirvana* extinction—attained by the Buddha after no less than 547 births. The goal of all existence in Christianity is to know God and enjoy Him forever. . . . Perhaps the greatest difference of all lies between the Bible which asserts that nobody can save himself and make himself pleasing to God, try as he will, and almost all the other faiths which assert that by keeping their teachings a man will be saved or re-born or made whole or achieve fulfillment.[1]

As well as sending out long-term missionaries, one of the great joys of our own church here in Nottingham is to see students, postgraduates, and others going out to South America, Africa, Europe, and the Far East as short-term workers in a host of situations for medical, social, and directly evangelistic work. Whether for a few months or one or two years, such an investment into God's work abroad can be of great value. Short-term workers are not to be despised. A short-term worker can end by becoming a long-term one! A short-term worker can give a long-term worker, or family, a much-needed vacation. A short-term worker can be used to train others in necessary skills from medicine to carpentry.

However, for every Christian the mission of the church involves home mission. Even if you never set foot in another land, your own mission field lies around you. You are crucially strategic to God's plans for the spread of His kingdom. There are people only you, of all Christians, will meet, places only you will go, opportunities only you will have. Your circle, at work or in the extended family, may have no other opportunity to hear the Good News of Jesus Christ clearly and personally. You may often experience rebuffs and discouragement, but you will also experience curiosity, openness, and a real desire to know God. You may be the only person they will ever talk to who knows God! Don't say, "Oh, my testimony is very ordinary, very unimpressive, very dull." That is, frankly, ludicrous. If God has stepped into your life, His activity will seem anything but dull to someone who has never known God. Just tell it as it is, without apology and with unashamed gratitude.

We often fear we will not be able to argue our own

case convincingly or answer the objections that are commonly raised against the Christian faith. Well, certainly, we Christians ought to study our faith in order to give good reason for the hope we have (1 Peter 3:15). However, when our *life* demonstrates the love and righteousness of God, we don't need to argue fiercely or to know all the answers. One of the best proofs of the Gospel of Jesus Christ is the changed characters and lives of His followers. When your life is a light, people won't ask you if there is a light but where you got it from!

God in heaven has a kingdom on earth. We belong to that kingdom because we have been called by the King, Jesus who is Lord. That kingdom is a growing kingdom. It has grown through twenty centuries and it is growing in our own. Yet its expansion is through us and not apart from us, and through us as we are and not just as we would like to be. In his book *Know and Tell the Gospel,* John Chapman writes:

> The hardest part of all evangelism is starting. We will do almost anything except begin. We do another training course, read another book. We form yet another committee and even go to a prayer meeting about it. But if you have not started—IT IS TIME. The best way to learn is to do it. None of us is much good at the beginning.[2]

Each morning before the work of the day begins, pray, "Who today, Lord?" "Where today, Lord?" "How today, Lord?" Every day will be different, but each day will have its possibilities and its significance. This is your part in the prayer "Your kingdom come"; and it is unique!

NOTES

1. Michael Green, *You Must Be Joking* (London: Hodder & Stoughton, 1981), 43.
2. John Chapman, *Know and Tell the Gospel* (London: Hodder & Stoughton, 1981), 104.

Chapter Twenty-One

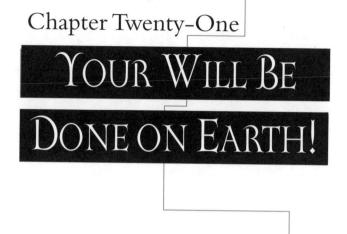

YOUR WILL BE DONE ON EARTH!

*J*esus tells us to pray "Your will be done on earth." It is, of course, a serious thing to pray that the whole world will be dominated by one will. Have we not seen terrible things done in totalitarian states where a particular ideology was imposed? Moreover, to many people it is an unwelcome and challenging thought that the individual's will should be subject to another's will. Does this mean that we should be unthinking, assembly-line creatures; mere items in a master plan? Does it mean the end of independence and even integrity, the end of self-fulfillment and the pursuit of happiness?

If by independence we mean a life independent of God (that is, as far as we *can* live it!), then certainly this must end whenever God asserts His lordship and wherever His name is hallowed. But the end of that kind of independence does not mean the end of individuality and true freedom. Rather, in God we find our uniqueness and true freedom to become what He wants us to be. God's will does not crush us into anonymity and a mass with others; it develops, directs, and guides us toward a full flowering of our God-intended beauty and usefulness in this world and the world to come. For God's will is not to be separated from His love, and what He wills for us will prove to be best for us. It is our wisdom to learn this.

I sometimes tell congregations the story of a large cargo of exotic South American birds that was being shipped to Europe many years ago for sale. During the voyage one of the birds got out of its cage. Efforts to recapture it in the hold only ended with its getting out to the deck and then escaping from the ship altogether. The sailors helplessly watched it fly triumphantly into the blue sky—free, free. ("Free as a bird," I suppose we might say!) They gave it up for lost and carried on with their tasks. However, a few days later the same bird reappeared and collapsed on deck, bedraggled and exhausted. It had discovered that there are not many trees in the mid-Atlantic! It had been "free" but found no rest; its freedom was fatal to its survival in a hostile environment.

So it is for human beings. We too take our flight into folly, insisting on our freedom to do our own thing and live without God, thinking, *He is, after all, so restrictive.* But our freedom leaves us exhausted and threatened in a fallen world. Satisfaction eludes us, rest is denied us, and hostile forces—time and chance, and death at the end—wait to defeat us. We may live in rebellion against God, but our freedom is fatal: it is the freedom of the bird that was made for the rain forests trapped in the mid-Atlantic. For life without boundaries, without guidance, without God becomes life without meaning or purpose or peace.

There is no prayer more right, more sure, more hopeful than the prayer "Your will be done"—for individuals and for societies. Men and women resent it, but we may ask what has opposition to God and His ways done for us in history and in the present? We have not gained by our stubbornness. The kingdoms of man have been failures and the self-worship of the individual is leading more and more to frustration, unhappiness, and even cruelty.

Only the kingdom of God is "righteousness and peace and joy in the Holy Spirit." To know God is the end of despair; to become His child is the beginning of hope; to enter His kingdom is to enter an abundant life; and to follow His will is the way of peace. We often read on the goods we buy: "Follow the maker's instructions." If we do not we should not be surprised to encounter breakdown and ruin of the best device. But our society, our race has been resisting, contravening, and modifying the Maker's instructions since the Fall, and we have not proved cleverer or wiser than God.

Someone has said, "History is a series of breakdowns on the road of progress." And none of our politics or philosophies or social sciences has been able to free us from our trouble. Why? Because we ourselves are our worst enemies. Our trouble is in our own hearts, not our systems.

And so it will continue to be as long as we say to God not "Your will be done" but "My will be done" or "Our will be done." Collectively and individually we are, in and of ourselves, hopelessly flawed. Only God, the God of hope, can rescue and remake us. The God whose will is done in heaven is the God whose will must be done on earth if earth is ever to be happy and men and women brought to fulfillment. So the church prays for herself and for the world, "Your will be done on earth as it is in heaven."

Chapter Twenty-Two

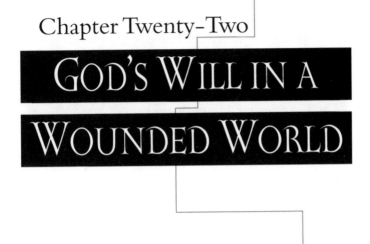

GOD'S WILL IN A WOUNDED WORLD

*Y*our will be done on earth as it is in heaven." We can never fully know God's "will" for this world, but we can seek and respond to it as it applies to our personal lives. A prayer like this can be understood in a number of ways. Here are four ways we can understand His "will" for our world, our nation, and our personal lives.

First, sometimes in Scripture God's "will" is His eternal purpose. This involves His decree and intentions, which are sure to come to pass because He is the omnipotent God. Thus His "will" most certainly will be done in the end, both in heaven and on earth. That is why the Old Testament could predict with confidence the coming of Christ and His kingdom even to a hostile and unpromising world, and the final triumph of good over evil. God was sovereign and His kingdom would triumph in "the day of the Lord." That too is why the New Testament can look forward with confidence to the triumph of Christ at His second coming, when He will set up the kingdom of heaven on a renewed earth, filling it with His goodness and His glory.

Second, sometimes God's "will" is His rule in a more present and direct way. His will includes His authority directing and controlling, His purposes coming to fruition in the present, His voice being heard among His people, and His church joyfully recognizing that God is enthroned in its midst, even in the old order of things. At such times God's will demonstrates openly, sometimes marvelously, the presence of the kingdom, as when Peter and John said to the cripple who asked for money, "Silver or gold I do not have, but what I have I give you. In the name of Jesus Christ of Nazareth, walk" (Acts 3:6). This rule is, as we can see, disputed and opposed in the world. It is, like the kingdom, only partially and provisionally here, but it is prophetically demonstrated in the life of the church where God's authority is recognized and His rule accepted.

Third, sometimes God's "will" is His grieving permission that we should share in the world's lot of suffering and loss. His ways do often lead through hard places in life. The problems around this are as old as the book of Job and as new as our own trials.

Sometimes for the Christian believer struggling through a world of evil and sorrow and pain, it is a prayer that has to be said in dark times when, like Jesus faced with the cross, we have to trust that God's will for us is best even when it means personal loss and suffering and even death.

God's way to our Easter morning often lies through a personal Gethsemane and beyond. At such times this is a prayer baptized in tears—tears that God knows and counts and shares. But He sees beyond the darkness and knows the plans He has for us beyond the dark clouds and in the glory. So it was with Christ who, for the joy that was set before Him, endured the cross.

Finally, when we pray this prayer for ourselves as individuals, God's will is the guidance we seek for our own lives. The way forward may be uncertain. How can we obtain the guidance of God to do His will? We pray for His wisdom and learn something of His plan for our lives, our careers, marriages, and homes. We need to pray, to look for principles of conduct in God's Word, to seek counsel from experienced and godly people. Yet even then we may be still unsure. Then it is that we must rest in the sovereignty of God as we tentatively move forward with this prayer still in our hearts. He is well able to recover the situation if we have made a wrong judgment, or to bring unexpected good out of our situation as things develop.

Our greatest duty is to seek His will in sincerity and self-giving, to trust His wisdom and love, and to obey His Word; and to leave the rest to a Father's care and kindness. What is of most importance is not that we do not know God's will in a situation or decision, but that we are *seeking* to know and do God's will in that particular matter.

It is there that we see what God has done in our lives already. We have been freed from the bondage of "my will be done," cured of the compulsion of "me first." Yes, we can still be selfish and foolish and uncaring, and there are disciplines yet to be acquired and desires yet to be conquered. But deep within our hearts is the cry, "Father, Thy will be done"; "Lord, take me, master me, make me all You want me to be."

Breathe on me, breath of God.
Fill me with life anew,
That I may love what thou cost
And do what thou wouldst do.

Breathe on me, breath of God,
Until my heart is pure;
Until my will is one with thine
To do and to endure.[1]

NOTE

1. Edwin Hatch (1835–1889), "Breathe on Me, Breath of God"; italics added for emphasis.

Chapter Twenty-Three

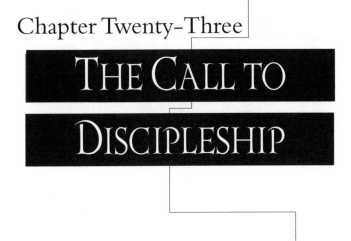

THE CALL TO
DISCIPLESHIP

God's will must be done "on earth" not only generally but in our own hearts and lives in particular. And in a fallen world where human wills are so commonly opposed to God's will, the surrender of our wills to Him is a significant and even dramatic event each and every time we do it. Each time we say, with sincerity and meaning, "Your will be done" we are bringing both the past and the future into the present. We are reliving that surrender to God which marked our first entrance into His kingdom, and we are bringing the future, when God's will shall be done throughout the earth, into the present. In that place, at that precise moment of prayer, the kingdom has come a little more and the end is a little nearer.

Yet it is not without resistance that the rule of the King extends itself into every part of our lives. We find it easy enough to say, "Your will be done," until that will clashes with ours, challenges ours, denies ours, and conquers ours. We are not used to having our will thwarted or our rights questioned. We were told that life is at our feet and now we must learn to lay it at God's feet. We were told that we must "go out there and make it happen," imposing our will on a situation, and now we must repeatedly yield up our will to God's will. This is not only a new way of thinking, it is also a new way of living, of acting and reacting, of planning and scrapping our plans.

It takes a lot of willpower to surrender our will. It needs the grace of God to yield to God's grace. But we only conquer when we surrender:

> My will is not my own
> Till Thou hast made it Thine;
> If it would reach the monarch's throne
> It must its crown resign:
> It only stands unbent,
> Amid the clashing strife,
> When on Thy bosom it has lent,
> And found in Thee its life.[1]

The call of Jesus is and always has been to discipleship. The Greek word for *disciple* is *mathetes,* which really means "learner." In the first-century world of the Gospels, every rabbi had his pupils, his learners, his disciples. They submitted to his teaching, to his "yoke" as the saying went (hence Jesus' words, "take my yoke upon you and learn from me" in Matthew 11:29). Thus a disciple was firstly *one who surrendered his judgment to his rabbi.* That was where all true discipleship had to start: learning from the teacher. In our case, we can learn from the best and wisest Teacher who ever lived, who knew God His

Father as no other knew or could know Him (Matthew 11:27), and whose life was the perfect commentary on His teaching. However, we cannot stop at that.

Our first duties as disciples of Christ are not only to listen to Him and to learn from Him but also to believe in Him. When His critics asked Jesus, "What must we do to do the works God requires?" He answered, "the work of God is this: to believe in the one he has sent" (John 6:28–29). Jesus called for faith and permanent self-giving. For Jesus is not among those teachers who talk and only require listeners, nor among those who philosophize and only produce theorists. He calls us to follow Him as Lord and Master, His willing servants, His faithful friends.

Doing God's will is the end and sign of all true religion (Matthew 7:21). As we are not to be hearers only (James 1:22), so we are not to be pray-ers only. Liturgy without lifestyle, the form of religion without the power and the practice of it, is everywhere in the Bible condemned as worthless. (See, for example, Isaiah 1:10–17; James 2:14–26.) The call of Christ is to faith and works, that is, to the faith *which* works. He calls us to serve our brothers and sisters, to bear fruit in love and good works and so demonstrate ourselves to be disciples indeed (see John 13:12–17; 15:8). Someone has said, "Jesus calls us down from the balcony where we are applauding Him to the dusty road where we must follow Him." And when we find ourselves weary, uncomfortable, and rejected, we must ask, not "Is it worth it?" but "Is *He* worth it?"

NOTE

1. George Matheson (1842–1906), "Make Me a Captive, Lord." In public domain.

Chapter Twenty-Four

NEED AND

OBEDIENCE

We live in an increasingly need-based society where our "needs," or what we think we need or what we are told we need, are the center point and the determining factor of personal morality and national economies. This has led to some unforeseen but not unforeseeable results. Our needs have grown steadily, our expectations have become unrealistic, and our feelings of disappointment have in many cases become savage. Our needs have become our rights, and if they are withheld we are presumed to have suffered injustice. We ourselves imagine ourselves to have been reduced if our needs remain unmet.

The effect of this has been startling and disturbing and far from our expectations. We are reduced by that very process which believes that we are only the sum of our needs and that the purpose of life is only to supply those needs. The meeting of needs becomes the process by which we become fully human.

In his book *All You Love Is Need,* Tony Walter suggests that we have moved from Descartes' "I think; therefore I am" to "I need; therefore I am."[1] These needs have become our starting point and our finishing point: You are what you eat/drive/wear/project. In this view "personality development is nothing but the meeting of personal needs, the economy is nothing but the meeting (or exploiting) of needs, marriage is nothing but the meeting of needs. . . . Need is the religion of the religionless, the morality of those who have progressed beyond morality."[2]

Christianity presents a startling contrast to this thinking, most powerfully by Jesus Christ Himself:

> The Christian faith is founded on a man whom Christians believe to be the most complete person this world has ever known. By present standards this man was poor in material things. He was not married, had no children and gave up his job in order to become an itinerant and unpaid preacher. The totalitarian Roman Empire in which he lived denied him many of those things which today are regarded as basic human needs. Moreover Jesus taught that far from basing our life on the needs of the self, we should take up our cross and deny our self.[3]

This does not mean, however, that human needs are irrelevant or that human beings are only to be assessed in "spiritual" or nonmaterial terms. Poverty *is* degrading and harmful; sickness and death are the enemy of us all; there are human rights as well as human wrongs. The harm is done when the supplying of every felt need becomes central and dominant, when the supplying of needs that are not in fact essential to human existence becomes the main reason for human existence, when rights are not balanced with responsibilities to others and become duty-less rights in a selfish and increasingly hedonistic society. It is from these things that our own affluent Western society is suffering.

And it is from such things that we in the church are suffering too! There is a great craving in this postmodern age for a religion which will fulfill us but not restrain us; which will give us all we lack but not take from us anything we want; which will leave our sin unchallenged and our conscience padded with comfort. We speak of "hurts" more than sins and present Jesus as the One people need if they are to be truly happy and fulfilled. Thomas A. Smail in *The Forgotten Father* has some salutary corrections to make in this regard:

> There is no doubt at all that for all of us much of the time it is our need that sets us running in a God-ward direction and God's grace consists precisely in the fact that he is ready to receive and deal with us on the basis of our need to supply it. But the purpose of Jesus is never just to meet people's needs, it is always when they come with their needs to make disciples, to attach people to himself so that they no longer want for themselves, but want to follow him more than they want anything for themselves.... [For disciples,] there has been a conversion from a need-based relationship to Jesus to an obedience-based relationship.[4]

This is the fundamental shift that conversion accomplishes in the heart and lives of believers. The centrality of my needs gives way to the centrality of His honor, His glory, His will. We move from "My will be done" to "Your will be done." This, however, is a process that needs to be affirmed and repeated daily in our lives as we say,

"Your will be done," not only in our world at large but in our lives in particular. This process runs counter to so much of our old thinking and lifestyle that a true surrender—not without struggle—has to be renewed repeatedly in our inner and outer lives.

We are to show the world what happens when God's will is done "on earth as it is in heaven" in our single lives and in our marriages, in our working lives, and in our church lives. As part of church communities headed by Christ and modeled on Christ, we must not only say in liturgy, "Lord, Lord," but do in life the will of our Father who is in heaven.

NOTES

1. Tony Walter, *All You Love Is Need* (London: SPCK, 1985), 154.
2. Ibid., 125.
3. Ibid., xiii.
4. Thomas A. Smail, *The Forgotten Father* (London: Hodder & Stoughton, 1987), 163–64.

Chapter Twenty-Five

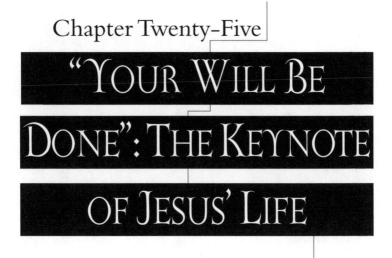

"YOUR WILL BE DONE": THE KEYNOTE OF JESUS' LIFE

*M*ore than any other figure in human history, Jesus Christ lived to fulfill the will of God His Father. That will was the map and mainspring of His life.

The writer of Hebrews captures the spirit in which Christ came into the world by using and quoting from one of the psalms: "Then I said, 'Here I am—it is written about me in the scroll—I have come to do your will, O God'" (10:7).

His coming into the world was an act of willing obedience, though it would cost Him dearly, as it cost the Father who "so loved the world that he gave"—to Bethlehem and to Calvary—this Son who "made himself nothing, taking the very nature of a servant" (Philippians 2:7). It was in servant form that He could say, "I have come down from heaven not to do my will but to do the will of him who sent me," and "I always do what pleases him" (John 6:38; 8:29). Jesus' obedience sprang from freedom, not restriction, noted J. I. Packer and Thomas

Howard: "Far from its having been a matter of 'knuck-ling under' to some tyrannical father-figure, Jesus said that His very 'meat' was to do His Father's will. In other words, He *enjoyed* His obedience: it was food and drink to Him; it brought Him strength and contentment; it left Him satisfied."[1]

The heartbeat of Jesus' obedience to the Father's will was love, and that love flowed out to those around Him in all their diversity and need: to the crowds who were as sheep without a shepherd, to the sick and the bereaved, to children and disciples (the latter sometimes being another kind of children), and to His enemies, even those who crucified Him. Love was His life, love His legacy, and love His rule (see John 15:9–12; Matthew 5:44).

From the life that loves issues the life that lives the prayer "Your will be done." That is the only possibility for authentic human existence:

> Now the rule or pattern, for our human life and hence for human freedom, says Christianity, is the rule of love. This is the will of God who called us into being. The point is, God is love and we are made in His image; which means, we have been made to live as He lives, doing at our level what He does at His. . . . We can find our fulfilment and joy only by loving as He loves, thus becoming increasing-ly like Him in personal moral practice. There is no con-tentment and therefore no freedom for human creatures if we try to live any other way.[2]

Beyond every other act of obedience in that life which lived to obey the Father who sent Him was Jesus' obedience unto "death—even death on a cross!" (Philip-pians 2:8). Here at the threshold of hell, of desolation and the curse, in full knowledge of the horrors in the cup He was given to drink, Jesus surrendered the last of His rights—the right to His Father's face. And so He prayed: "Father, if you are willing, take this cup from me; yet not my will, but yours be done" (Luke 22:42).

The will of God may be expected to lead to heaven —but not to hell! Yet the Lord of Glory becomes the outlaw and crosses the boundary line of all comfort into the desolation and anguish of hell, where there is no comfort. And He goes because it is His Father's will. He was the sinless Son, innocent of offense, "Yet it was the Lord's will to crush him and cause him to suffer" (Isaiah 53:10).

Why? Has God become vindictive, shall the Judge of all the earth do wrong?

> But he was pierced for our transgressions, he was crushed for our iniquities; the punishment that bought us peace was upon him, and by his wounds we are healed. We all, like sheep, have gone astray, each of us has turned to his own way; and the Lord has laid on him the iniquity of us all. (Isaiah 53:5–6)

It was thus that Christ fulfilled the "must" of prophecy under which He had consciously lived His whole life (see Luke 2:49; 22:37; 24:25–27, 44). His final act of obedience was of a piece with the rest of His life, yet it was also the final and chief reason for His coming into the world. Yet though it was "the Lord's will to crush him," "it was impossible for death to keep its hold on him" (Acts 2:24). He was led to the grave, but He was not left there. After the finished work, the full reward; the end of sufferings is the beginning of conquests. The will of God which crushed Him on earth carried Him to heaven, the risen, exalted Son, victorious over sin and death and hell. Indeed, "God exalted him to the highest place and gave him the name that is above every name" (Philippians 2: 9).

NOTES

1. J. I. Packer and Thomas Howard, *Christianity: The True Humanism* (Waco, Tex.: Word, 1985), 65.
2. Ibid., 66–67.

PART THREE

"GIVE US TODAY
OUR DAILY BREAD"

Chapter Twenty-Six

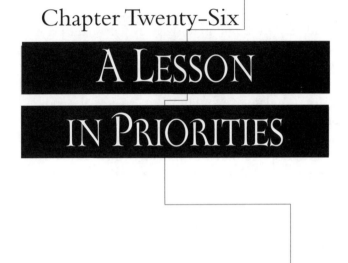

A LESSON
IN PRIORITIES

The words hardly strike us as dramatic, but they surely are: "Give us this day our daily bread." In one breath we speak of "our heavenly Father," and in the next "our daily bread"; one moment it is "your will" and in the next "my food." We move in the same solemn, exalted prayer from "infinities and immensities" to our weekly shopping and the loaf on the table!

Here are lessons about God and about us: lessons in His care and competence and lessons in our dependence and trust. He does not forget our humanity; we must not forget His divinity. He is a caring Father; we must be grateful children.

The place of this petition in the whole prayer is significant in more than one respect: it gives us first of all a lesson in priorities. Notice that it does not *begin* the Lord's Prayer. The prayer begins with God's glory and only later deals with our needs. It is most definitely "Hallowed be your name" before it is "Give us our daily bread." We are taught in this way, by Christ, the priorities of prayer. We so easily and so often begin with ourselves when we should begin with God. We bring shopping lists to the Throne as if God were a grocer, as if He existed for us and not we for Him. But "Man's chief end [purpose] is to glorify God and to enjoy Him forever," declares the Westminster Shorter Catechism.

We displace much of that enjoyment of God with the demands of life. We say, "Give us this" and "Give us that" and "Give us the other" until we are prayed out, and there is no room for "Give us Yourself" above all and, if it must be, instead of all. As Charles Wesley wrote, "Thou, O Christ, art all I want; / More than all in Thee I find."[1]

Yes, God does answer our prayers. But how can we expect answers to prayers we do not pray? Is our problem that God does give us what we ask for but not what we do *not* ask for? If that is often the case, then it is not surprising that so many Christians in our materialistic society are materially affluent but spiritually impoverished. We have what we want most—bread—but not blessing! Is it surprising that God should hesitate to give us what we do not sufficiently value? And can we say we greatly value what we leave to the end of the list? We make sure we are well stocked up each week from the neighborhood supermarket but live on iron rations when it comes to spiritual food obtained from prayer and the study of the Scriptures. Jesus too needed "daily bread," but as to supreme priorities He could say firmly, "My food is to do the will of him who sent me" (John 4:34).

Our Lord Jesus tells us that not bread but *God* is the "one thing needed" (Luke 10:42). To possess not only bread but the farms that supply it, and the factories that bake it, and the outlet stores that retail it, and the millions that customers pay for it, but not to have the Giver who gave it, is to be poor while rich and empty while full; it is to live on the scraps of the divine life.

It is true that we have all, at some time, burst into the presence of God in great fear or urgent need, and it is the measure of His fatherly love and understanding that He does not cast us back but embraces us and tenderly comforts us. Yet while even the psalmist does this, comfort does not come with real and lasting effect until he realizes what *God* is and dwells on that for a while in praise and love, and *then* comes to his problem. (See, for example, Psalms 71, 73, 77.)

Always remember that God is more important than your troubles, and insist on giving Him the place in all your prayers that He has in all the universe. The effect of this will not be to diminish you or your needs but to diminish your fears. It is when we begin with God in prayer that we get other things in perspective. Our immediate needs and fears retire to their right place; our fears dwindle before God's all-sufficiency. We are no longer lost in the crowd of events, because with the recognition of who God is comes the recollection of who we are. Then we can bring the problem to Him and lay our needs before Him, not in panic, but in reverence and quiet trust; then we can rise up and face the situation as we ought, whether the pantry is empty or full.

NOTE

1. Charles Wesley (1707–88), "Jesus, Lover of My Soul." In public domain.

Chapter Twenty-Seven

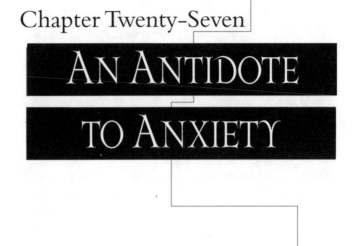

AN ANTIDOTE

TO ANXIETY

$\mathcal{W}$hen Jesus prayed, "Give us today our daily bread," He was linking the spiritual with the physical. Our Father in heaven cares—about things small and great, about the temporal as well as the eternal. The world of Jesus' day had as many agonies and uncertainties as the world of our day:

> The standard wage for a labourer in Jesus' day was a silver denarius a day. This was barely enough to keep a small family at subsistence level. If such a labourer did not find work for several days, his family was destitute. In such circumstances the fourth petition in the Lord's Prayer ("Give us today our bread for this day") takes on a poignancy many of us no longer experience. It is a prayer for survival.[1]

Yet Jesus, in the Sermon on the Mount, urged His followers not to be consumed with anxiety: "Therefore I tell you, do not worry about your life, what you will eat or drink; or about your body, what you will wear" (Matthew 6:25). And He bases our peace on a relationship with a heavenly Father who knows and cares; one who feeds "the birds of the air" and clothes "the lilies of the field" and values His children who have a much more glorious destiny than birds or flowers (6:26–30). To be obsessed with material as opposed to spiritual necessities is to live like those who acknowledge no heavenly Father (6:32). It is to reverse the priorities of the kingdom. "But seek first his kingdom and his righteousness, and all these things will be given to you as well," Jesus said (6:33).

Yet we immediately have a problem with such promises—and it is in part a very modern problem. We, in our time, have been encouraged to challenge everything, always to look for the exception, always to stress the negative.

We have made cynicism a virtue. The psalmist could say, "I was young and now I am old, yet I have never seen the righteous forsaken or their children begging bread" (37:25). Well, we could show him a thing or two! Give us the streets of Calcutta or Mexico City, a video camera and a time machine, and we'll fill the gaps in his experience! But this is to miss his point. He too lives in "the real world." But he has learned to count blessings as well as ironies, to see the positive as well as the negative, and to see (as often those believers who have lived through hard times have seen) that while we are not immune to the tragedies and inequities of life in a fallen world, yet we are not alone in that world nor abandoned to it. Soon the psalmist's spiritual descendants would learn of a God whose Son became a refugee at the beginning of His earthly life and a crucified victim of injustice at its end. Did God not care *then?* Was he uninvolved *there?*

We too sometimes fall victims to life's violence, tragedy, and unfairnesses. Nevertheless, for most of us most of the time, the famous words of Psalm 91 are true: not as blank checks but as day-passes through the dangers of life: "He [she] who dwells in the shelter of the Most High will rest in the shadow of the Almighty.... If you make the Most High your dwelling—even the Lord, who is my refuge—then no harm will befall you, no disaster will come near your tent" (Psalm 91:1, 9–10).

And when it does, when the evil day comes, when the sparrow falls out of the nest and evil slays the good, the sacred sovereignty of God is still at work. Our Father knows the hairs of our head are all numbered; we are not abandoned, our worth is not diminished (see Matthew 10:30–31).

Here is a lesson in trust and an invitation to peace—even in the midst of dangers and in the process of struggle. The apostle Paul urged us to learn this lesson when he wrote: "Do not be anxious about anything, but in everything, by prayer and petition, with thanksgiving, present your requests to God. And the peace of God, which transcends all understanding, will guard your hearts and your minds in Christ Jesus" (Philippians 4:6–7).

Sometimes anxiety can be a kind of atheism. Our fears or problems fill the horizon until God is given no place; our worries are everywhere and God is nowhere. But He calls us to prayer, not to an escape from everything but to prayer "in everything." Prayer is not escapism; it is a unique kind of involvement. Our engagement with life as it is does not change, but we who engage with it are changed. We are still occupied with our problems but no longer obsessed with them. Prayer precedes our daily conflict, peace remains in that conflict at deep levels, and at night we can, in thanksgiving, remember our Father's involvement and transcendence. We can rest in His concern and His sovereignty, His deliverances in the past and His promises about the future.

NOTE

1 David Bosch, *Transforming Mission* (Maryknoll, N.Y.: Orbis, 1991), 27.

Chapter Twenty-Eight

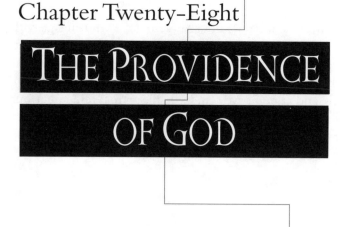

THE PROVIDENCE

OF GOD

*G*od's providence is in large measure His "provide-
ence," as the English word suggests. He is indeed the
God who provides. In the psalmist's words:

> The Lord is faithful to all his promises
>   and loving toward all he has made.
> The Lord upholds all those who fall
>   and lifts up all who are bowed down.
> The eyes of all look to you,
>   and you give them their food at the proper time.
> You open your hand and satisfy the desires
>   of every living thing. (Psalm 145:13–16)

In the famous words of our Lord Jesus, God our
heavenly Father feeds the birds, dresses the lilies, and
clothes the grass of the field (see Matthew 6:25–30). This
is not a blind romanticism. Jesus recognizes the trouble
of life and its effects, but He recognizes too the constant
work of God sustaining a damaged earth—damaged in

its ecology and its humanity. And of course, as we have seen, He recognizes God's special concern for His own children, the children of the kingdom, the ones who daily pray this prayer because they have a relationship with God the provider, as their Father in heaven.

The provision prayed for here takes place precisely in a world of uncertainty, of inequity, and of spoliation; of failed crops, of famine, and of war. The psalmist and his Lord both live in the same world as we do. But they do not blame God for its ills. Ours is a world that is not simply the world God made; it is also one that we have made. It is a world where there is food enough for all but where war has despoiled huge tracts of fertile land, where greed has exploited natural resources, and where selfishness has unfairly distributed God's provision. History is marked by the failure of human beings, not of God: "The fault, dear Brutus, is not in our stars but in ourselves."[1] But it is also a world marked by the sovereign providence of God.

The Bible never allows us to relinquish our hold on the sovereignty of God. From first to last, God is sovereign. He created the world in its beginning, He will redeem it in the end, and He overrules it in the meantime (see Isaiah 45:1–7).

There are great mysteries here, to be sure; the mystery of providence being one of the greatest. How can God be sovereign over a world that sidelines His existence, flouts His laws, and violates His will? How can God be sovereign and human beings be free and responsible agents? We can see how a god can be good and not all-powerful, so that evil becomes, as in so many old religions and philosophies, an equal and opposite "force" to good. We can see how a god can be all-powerful but not all-good, having, as in some other dualistic systems, a dark as well as a light side. But to reconcile the God of the Bible with the world of the newspapers, that is hard: "God Almighty and ills unlimited." He is a God altogether good who does not prevent things altogether bad in our world—which is also His. A God who gives daily bread to millions in a world where millions more go undernourished or many starve to death.

We cannot make sense of all this—and neither does the Bible. Nor does it try! Indeed, it is a question whether we can make "sense" of sin which is nonsense, contrary to God's order, to life's truth and to our good. Sin has brought chaos to our world; our racial Fall brought "death into the world, and all our woe," as Milton put it in *Paradise Lost*. But though sin brought many evils into the world, it did not expel God from the world! The God who cast Adam and Eve out of the Garden also went with them out of the Garden. The God who devastated the world in Noah's day also began a new chapter in salvation history in Abraham's day. The God who cursed the earth because of human sin also entered that world "in the likeness of sinful man" and bore its curse in Himself, that those condemned might be forgiven and justified and become heirs of God's future for the world we spoiled (Romans 8:1–4; see also Galatians 3:13). The same God now, as ever, works increasingly in love and pain in this sinful world to call men and women to Himself in repentance and faith (see Acts 17:30–31). The ills of a fallen world are not unlimited. The day will come when there will be "no more death or mourning or crying" for the old, fallen, spoiled order of things will have passed away (Revelation 21:4).

Holy Scripture therefore faces *both* realities: God's goodness *and* mankind's cruelties, God's justice *and* life's inequalities, God's righteousness *and* our unrighteousness. It does not cover up sin, even in the best of its characters; and it does not compromise the righteousness of God, even in the worst of their sufferings.

We often hear of Auschwitz in this regard, and the terrible holocaust of the last war, as if there could no longer be talk of providence or omnipotence or even God. You would sometimes think God had built Auschwitz instead of suffering in its horrors! Israel in Isaiah's day and Judah in Jeremiah's day also had their holocausts; yet the prophets stood firm in the midst of all their tears and heartbreak. (For example, see Lamentations 3:1–33.) And so must we.

More crucially still, the worst deed in all of human history, the crucifixion of the Son of God, was said to have taken place under God's sovereignty and not at the cost of it. On the day of Pentecost the apostle Peter preached to the crowd about Jesus: "This man was handed over to you by God's set purpose and foreknowledge; and you, with the help of wicked men, put him to death by nailing him to the cross" (Acts 2:23). Here was an act of inexcusable human wickedness ("You . . . put him to death") that was ordained "by God's set purpose" and prefigured in Old Testament sacrifices and prophecies (for example, Psalm 22:1–31; Isaiah 53:6, 10). How, in this or in any subsequent event, God can seriously yet sinlessly ordain and overrule the free acts of human beings is a mystery beyond philosophy and beyond our little logic. But the writers of Scripture held fast to the goodness and sovereignty of God and to the culpability of a rebellious race and wicked people in it. He who gave them life will judge them in the end, and as His forgiveness now is mighty so His wrath then will be terrible.

Meantime, His people rely on His sovereignty for their confidence that He will triumph in the end (see Habakkuk 2:3), that His kingdom will come, and that the earth will in that day "be filled with the knowledge of the glory of the Lord, as the waters cover the sea" (Habakkuk 2:14). We have His word for it!

Equally, that sovereign overruling secretly persists in a world in which countless things are done to God's dishonor and pain. He never made a child cry or a prisoner scream. He is life not death, a Father not a fiend, and He calls us to turn to Him, to trust Him (see James 1:17), to follow Him. Every good gift comes from Him, and He still sends His rain "upon the righteous and the unrighteous" (Matthew 5:45), but He does so to give us space for repentance before a judgment which will come soon enough (see 2 Peter 3:8–9).

Meanwhile, He continues to be God, creator, sustainer, provider and above all savior. He is also Father, Son, and Spirit, to whom His children can look for provision and protection in redeemed lives that have their appointed destiny in Him. Those lives are governed even now, not by blind fate but by a farsighted providence that sees our future joys and steadfastly leads us to them. He is every day and every hour the God who can work in all things, great and small, in all events, good and bad, in all people, reconciled and hostile, "for the good of those who love him, who have been called according to his purpose" (Romans 8:28). This has been the glad experience of God's people from Joseph in the Old Testament to Paul in the New (see Genesis 45:4–11; Philippians 1:12–14). It is the provision of God that covers the lifestyle of the sparrow and counts the hairs of our heads. It is the concern of Jehovah Jireh—our provider.

NOTE

1. William Shakespeare, *Julius Caesar* 1.2. 140–41. Cassius bemoans to Brutus their lesser authority compared with that of Caesar.

Chapter Twenty-Nine

AN INVITATION
TO CONTENTMENT

There is an old story about an English lord who was passing the kitchens in his stately home one day and heard his cook, clearly distressed, say to her assistant, "Oh, if only I had five pounds." Because he appreciated her work, he walked into the room and gave the astonished woman five pounds in cash. Then he pretended to leave the area but hung around within earshot to catch her reaction. When she thought he had gone, he heard her say in exasperated tones to her companion, "Drat it! If I'd known, I'd have said fifty!"

Contentment is not something that comes easily to us. Nor is it something that we find easy to keep when we have it. We speak of "finding contentment" as if it lay waiting to be discovered or hiding elusively while we hunt for it. We are sure that we will be content in the next job or the next house, or with the next car or the new furniture. But, like the carrot tied to the donkey, it will always be just out of reach for as long as we think of it in that way.

For contentment depends on an inner quality, not just on an outward condition. It rises within us from a recognition that what we have is more valuable than what we do not have, and that what we lack in ourselves can never be made up from what we may acquire in the world around us.

The apostle Paul makes just this point when he tells his Philippian readers:

> I have learned to be content whatever the circumstances. I know what it is to be in need, and I know what it is to have plenty. I have learned the secret of being content in any and every situation, whether well fed or hungry, whether living in plenty or in want. I can do everything through him who gives me strength. (4:11–13)

The word translated "content" was used in the ancient world by the philosophers to describe the self-sufficient man, the man who made himself independent of circumstances and had sufficient strength within himself to meet all circumstances calmly. Hence the New English Bible translation of verse 11, "I have learned to find resources in myself whatever my circumstances." Unlike the philosophers, however, Paul traces this self-sufficiency to the indwelling Spirit of Christ; as he puts it, "I can do everything through him who gives me strength" (4:13). Bible commentator Peter O'Brien notes: "He was not so much self-sufficient as God-sufficient."[1]

There are lessons here for us all. Every man and woman lives in two worlds—an external world and an internal world. The external world is the world of action;

the internal world is the world of identity. Often, however, we confuse these two worlds and "find" our identity solely in the external world of actions and circumstances. A man or woman gets wealth, power, and prestige in the outer world and imagines that he or she is that image, that reputation, that lifestyle. The individual places his identity in his success, promotion, popularity, or luxury. Then, when the person is stripped of these (or fails to achieve them), he becomes disoriented or dismayed; he or she may suffer an identity crisis. The person's resources were all outside himself, and when these were taken away there was nothing left from which to draw comfort, support, and reassurance.

But this is tragic, and the more so because it is unnecessary. The man and the woman are in themselves so much more important and significant than all those other things. We are always bigger than our gains, bigger than our successes—or lack of success.

One believer who had been rich and then, through no fault of his own, had lost everything, still retained his joy and peace as a Christian. When asked how he could remain so much the same after his misfortune as before it, he replied with beautiful wisdom: "When I was rich I had God in everything. Now that I am poor I have everything in God." That was Paul's triumph and it can be ours.

This does not mean, of course, that our outward lives and their achievements are unimportant. God gives us gifts, and we should use them. God gives success in many things at many points in our lives, and we can celebrate it. It is neither natural nor spiritual to be indifferent to success or failure, and Paul does not say otherwise. He learned not to be *indifferent* but to be *content,* and there is a world of difference between the two. He is a grateful, trusting Christian, not a passionless stone!

Nor does this mean that the losses and crosses of life are easy to bear. The grace of contentment is not an anesthetic that numbs the pains of life, but an attitude that can cope with life's losses and its gains, its burdens and its comforts. This mind-set and spirit is learned only gradually and sometimes painfully.

Paul makes clear that this was his own experience. Twice he says, "I have learned" this, "I have learned the secret." No doubt Paul, the man of action, had often chafed at delay; no doubt with the expectations of zeal he had found it as hard as any of us would to deal equally with disgrace and honor. Character, like coral, is built up only little by little. It is by a thousand small victories that the war is won. How we meet each day's events, pressures, and opportunities; how we respond to events we cannot control (for while events may lie beyond our control, our response to them does not); and how the experiences of life, good and bad, leave us, will determine whether we, as the years unfold, will have learned what Paul learned. If we do, we shall have learned a valuable lesson. We shall be rich, not poor; we shall have acquired what an old writer calls "the rare jewel of Christian contentment."

As to the supply of our daily needs: just as we have learned that God is aware of them, that He is concerned about them, that He has been supplying them on a pretty regular basis for millions of us, every day and through long years, so we can look to Him and rest in Him to continue to do what He has so graciously and lovingly and faithfully done. Our daily bread is not to be our daily worry, even if it is our daily prayer.

However, there is one more thing to be said in this regard: this prayer is for our need, not our greed. It is not a prayer for the finest wines or the richest cuisine but for the basics of life. These may be our legitimate concern—the rest is God's to give but not ours to expect. "Having food and raiment let us be therewith content" (1 Timothy 6:8 KJV). Such an attitude comes most easily from those who know how little they deserve and how much they have been forgiven. For while this is "the children's prayer," it is the prayer of sinners too. How impudent are our "shopping list prayers," as we ask for this and expect that and almost demand the other! To be sure, God is not begrudging in His forgiveness, and our justification is complete in Christ. Yet as those who are still tottering in their holy walk, stammering and stumbling in their conversations with their Father, sinfully anxious one hour and sinfully confident the next, we need to learn the humility that seeks not what we want but what God wants for us. God knows what we can cope with, what is best for His glory and for our good.

I have long valued the wisdom in this prayer of an old churchman—and often smiled at the last line:

> Lord, though such temporal enjoyments may seem good and desirable to me at present, yet thou art infinitely wise and knowest what the consequence of them will be. I ask for them if they may stand with thy will and if thou seest they will be as really good for me as I suppose them to be. If they be not so, I beg the favour of a denial.[2]

Have you learned to "beg the favor of a denial?"

NOTES

1. Peter O'Brien, *The Epistle to the Philippians* (Grand Rapids: Eerdmans, 1991), 521.
2. Ezekiel Hopkins, *Works* (London: n.p., 1701), 751.

Chapter Thirty

AN INVITATION
TO OUTRAGE

*E*very year 13 million children under the age of five die, many of hunger-related causes. Worldwide 190 million children under five are severely malnourished. More than one-fifth of the world's population (one billion human beings) is without adequate food, safe water, basic health care and primary education. There is sufficient food in the world for everyone to receive about 2,500 calories each day, but many people are unable to buy the food, and distribution of supplies is grossly unequal.

God has given enough food on this planet to feed everyone; enough energy to serve everyone; enough people, power, and progress to reach everyone. Given our world as it is, however, the problems of meeting worldwide need are immense. The greatest enemies remain apathy and despair, selfishness and greed, hatred and war. The roots of these lie in the heart of all mankind. The problem is not a God who does not care but a race that will not share.

Corruption and sin are not only in one place. The West has blushed at its butter mountains and meat mountains, its wine lakes, its milk poured away and its wheat stocks burned, and at its economic explanations and moral discomfort. Yet many underdeveloped countries have leaders (the "lootocracy") who siphon off economic aid to keep their "gangs" and armies happy; marketeers who steal and sell food that was given freely; unbribed officials who leave food rotting on docksides while populations starve inland.

Poverty due to political maladministration, social bias, and lack of opportunity offends God, degrades people, and should outrage the Christian. Systems do need to be reformed, prejudice does need to be corrected, indifference does need to be challenged. And the Christian church and individual Christians in the marketplace and in high places of influence and trust should be outstanding and outspoken in their generation. In his book on Amos, Roy Clements writes:

> We have got to get out of the individualistic cast of mind.... We are part of a world that has gone wrong and we share its guilt. A religion that is obsessed with personal holiness but which is content to let society go to the dogs is not based on true repentance; it is just self-indulgent pietism.... There has to be that social dimension to our repentance.[1]

John Stott notes three types of "poor" in Old Testament life: *the indigent poor,* who are deprived of the basic necessities of life; *the oppressed poor,* who are powerless victims of human injustice; and *the humble poor,* who acknowledge their helplessness and look to God for salvation. Here economic, sociological, and spiritual categories may overlap. The lessons of the Bible are that God sees, understands, and reacts to these conditions. To quote Stott: "God succours the indigent poor, champions the powerless poor and exalts the humble poor."[2]

The challenge to us is that He seeks to do this through us. Stott insists that in the light of biblical revelation and in the sight of worldwide poverty, Christians must modify their lifestyles: "We cannot maintain a 'good life' [of extravagance] and a 'good conscience' simultaneously. One or another has to be sacrificed."[3]

Stott does not call us to artificial or unrealistic extremes, but he does call us to cultivate generosity, simplicity, and contentment. Similarly, Paul does not command us to artificial or unrealistic extremes, but he does command us to generosity when he writes to Timothy: "Command those who are rich in this present world not to be arrogant nor to put their hope in wealth. . . . Command them to do good, to be rich in good deeds, and to be generous and willing to share" (1 Timothy 6:17–18).

An age-old response to this among God's people has been the tithe: the devotion of one-tenth (and more in the Old Testament economy) of one's income to religious and charitable purposes. It began as a point of honor with Abraham, became a matter of Israelite law under Moses, and remains, I believe, as an evangelical challenge in this gospel age. In the New Testament we are encouraged to give not out of legal obligation but as a glad and grateful response (see 2 Corinthians 8:1–5) to the complete self-giving of Christ, who "though he was rich, yet for your sakes he became poor" (2 Corinthians 8:9). Such giving brings glory to God and the blessing of those helped upon those who have helped them (see 2 Corinthians 9:12–14).

Yet beyond regular giving a needy world calls for extraordinary times of giving too. Our TV screens in recent years have shown us terrible scenes of hunger and distress, from Ethiopia to Rwanda. It is a time for extraordinary response from governments and individuals, as potbellied children cry out of our screens to us, "Give us today our daily bread!"

No doubt we feel very helpless before the enormity of the problem, and God does not lay upon us the evil of the world. He does call us, however, to work with Him to alleviate its misery for someone, somewhere, in some way.

Once a freak ocean wave cast hundreds of fish on a stretch of shoreline. One man was seen desperately running from one to another, carrying them to the safety of the water. "But there are hundreds!" cried a passerby. "What difference can you hope to make?" The man replied, "Well, it's made all the difference in the world to the ones I've rescued!"

NOTES

1. Roy Clements, *Where Love and Justice Meet* (Leicester, England: InterVarsity, 1988), 81.
2. John Stott, *Issues Facing Christians Today* (Basingstoke, England: Marshalls, 1984), 220.
3. Ibid., 226.

PART FOUR

"FORGIVE US OUR DEBTS
AS WE ALSO HAVE FORGIVEN
OUR DEBTORS"

Chapter Thirty-One

OUR

PROBLEM

*O*ur Lord's model prayer now moves from bread to forgiveness. Jesus takes us from what is essential for physical life to what is essential for eternal life. Here He reminds us of our greatest dignity and our greatest danger: namely, that we were made for eternal fellowship with God our creator but we have sinned and made ourselves liable to His wrath as judge. Yet He does not leave us under condemnation, but gives us a prayer that carries with it an implicit readiness in God to forgive and to restore us to our first destiny.

"Forgive us our debts as we also have forgiven our debtors." Without forgiveness, our lives would indeed be lived under the shadow of a great despair. What would bread be without forgiveness—or riches or power or prestige or long life be without peace with God? In Jesus' unforgettable words to the disciples: "What is a man profited, if he shall gain the whole world, and lose his own soul?" (Matthew 16:26 KJV).

An essential characteristic of the Christian message is the unique stress it lays upon the matter of sin: its nature and its descents, its seriousness and its effects, and God's way of salvation in Christ Jesus. That message begins, "All have sinned and fall short of the glory of God" and ends with, "God made him who had no sin to be sin for us, so that in him we might become the righteousness of God" (Romans 3:23; 2 Corinthians 5:21). J. I. Packer writes:

> If you have not learned about sin, you cannot understand yourself or your fellow men, or the world in which you live or the Christian faith. And you will not be able to make head or tail of the Bible. For the Bible is an exposition of God's answer to the problem of human sin, and unless you have that problem clearly before you, you will keep missing the point of what it says.[1]

Looking at human history, our daily newspapers, and our own hearts, we feel a growing puzzlement and exasperation: We just can't "get it right." The Bible reveals why. It's our sin.

The Scriptures represent the sinful state of men and women by many different pictures or metaphors. For instance, we are said to be:

> *polluted* by our sin, needing to be washed
> *in slavery* to sin, needing to be freed
> *asleep* in our sins, needing to be awakened
> *diseased* by sin, needing to be healed
> *dead* in sin, needing to be raised

In all these figures of speech the message is clear: We cannot help or save ourselves; we need nothing less than

God to save us. Here in the Lord's Prayer we are said to be *debtors* on account of sin, utterly unable to pay what we owe. God's free forgiveness is our only hope.

This is a debt that burdens everyone, God's goodness notwithstanding. We are debtors but not because God is a hard taskmaster or creditor. James reminds his readers that "every good and perfect gift" is from "the Father of the heavenly lights" (James 1:17). However, our racial godlessness and past rebellion, our thoughtlessness and casual ingratitude have long since turned *gifts* into *debts*, daily bread into daily contraband, blessings stolen and traded in lives that are alienated from the rule of God.

We still speak of a person's "debt" to society when he or she is imprisoned for breaking the law of the land. Scripture tells us that God too has a law: not an arbitrary or even utilitarian code of required behavior, but a law proceeding from His own essential being and nature as "holy." God's law proceeding from His righteousness, justice, and truth requires perfect obedience. We, His unique creation, owe Him all obedience in thought and word and deed: glad recognition of His goodness, willing conformity to His standards. This is what we owe, what unfallen angels give as the very stuff of their existence, but what we are now disabled from doing by our own fault and folly, both individually and as a race (see Romans 3:9–20; 5:12).

We have transgressed that law times without number and the burden of our debts has grown by the year. Sin unrepented and unforgiven does not diminish with time any more than old debts unpaid, which in fact grow with interest. Like unscrupulous businessmen, we may hide our bankruptcy behind a facade of talent, style, and achievements, but none of them can deal with or even diminish the huge bill of debts we have run up with God our maker and our judge.

Our sins affect others too. No one sins for himself alone. Our dishonesties cheat others, our immoralities corrupt and compromise others, theft and violence leave scars on the mind as well as the body.

The effects of sin spread wider than we like to think. As factory and industrial smoke in England can kill trees in Norway by producing acid rain, so one generation's permissive and cynical fashions in morality and gross materialism can corrupt another, polluting its young growth with the acids of their own callous selfishness, sick humor, and amoral propaganda.

None of us knows the total effect of our sins or indeed of any particular sin for, as Paul Tournier has somewhere put it, "The high drama of evil is that it cannot be localized." It is such thoughts as these that bring us to our knees—and to our Savior.

NOTE

1. J. I. Packer, *God's Words* (Leicester, England: InterVarsity, 1981), 71.

Chapter Thirty-Two

GOD'S

SOLUTION

The gospel is about God's solution to humanity's greatest problem. That problem was entirely ours in respect of sin and guilt, but God made it His in respect of forgiveness and reconciliation. That God should love is not surprising, for God is love. That God should love sinners is astonishing, for God is holy and God's holiness includes His utter incompatibility with anything corrupt or unrighteous in His creation. As we consider in depth Jesus' words "Forgive us our debts," we must ask: How can God love sinners? How can God forgive sins, be just, and be the one "who justifies the ungodly" (Romans 4:5 RSV)?

John Stott, in *The Cross of Christ,* quotes Carnegie Simpson, "Forgiveness to man is the plainest of duties; to God it is the profoundest of problems," and carefully unpacks the second half of that statement:

> The obstacle to forgiveness is neither our sin alone, nor our guilt alone, but also the divine reaction in love and

wrath towards guilty sinners. For, although indeed "God is love", yet we have to remember that his love is "holy love", love which yearns over sinners while at the same time refusing to condone their sin. How, then, could God express his holy love? . . . Confronted by human evil, how could God be true to himself as holy love?[1]

The astonishing message of the New Testament is that God Himself in holy love took personal responsibility for all our sins—for the payment of all our debts—to satisfy His own justice. In the words of John Stott again, "He bore the judgment we deserve in order to bring us the forgiveness we do not deserve."[2]

The cross of Calvary is the focal point of that work. There He died, "the righteous for the unrighteous, to bring you to God" (1 Peter 3:18). There He became "the atoning sacrifice for our sins, and not only for ours but also for the sins of the whole world" (1 John 2:2).

The reconciliation that flows from that act and its achievement is the central proclamation of the New Testament. As Paul says, "God was reconciling the world to himself in Christ, not counting men's sins against them. And he has committed to us the message of reconciliation" (2 Corinthian 5:19).

People sometimes ask, "Why do we need to pray for forgiveness each day if we are forgiven our sins from the start of our new life in Christ? Isn't our first forgiveness enough?"

Truly if that first forgiveness is not enough for our eternal salvation, and if our justification is incomplete at our first entry into Christ as His people, then we could have no peace or joy as Christians, only fear and trepidation and anxiety. We would be afraid every day of losing our salvation; anxious that we had failed to maintain some standard. But that is not the New Testament picture of the Christian life, which is to be a life of assurance, joyful certainty that whatever happens to us we are safe in God, saved in Christ His Son.

Well, then, what do we as believers have here in the daily prayer "Forgive us our sins"? Not a reference to our definitive state of salvation, but a reference *within that* to our state of closeness to God, cleanness before God, communion with God (see John 13:10; 14:23). The forgiveness sought is not the removal of damnation but the restoration of fellowship with God. For sin is of such a nature and God is of such a nature that, though He will not now damn us because of our sins, He will and does chastise us for our sins. And for us the worst chastisement of all is to feel His absence, to sense His grief and anger (see Psalm 51:7–12).

For the true Christian it is not enough to be saved from hell. We want to walk with God, to be close to God. But our sins disturb that intimacy, and may disturb our peace. We do not cease to be children of God—we can still pray "Our Father"—but we are like children locked out, kept at a distance, the show of affection withdrawn. And so we pray "forgive us our sins" as a much-loved child comes in sorrow to be drawn close by a loving parent. Mere forgiveness is not enough—we want forgiveness with kisses, forgiveness and our Father's face.

Second, people are often puzzled by the additional words ". . . as we also have forgiven our debtors." Is this an attempt at a trade-off, our forgiveness of others traded for God's forgiveness of us? Of course not. It can't be. Our forgiveness is always incomplete: We are sinners in everything. And certainly we cannot *earn* forgiveness at any level. Salvation is all of grace. It is free. It is God's gift.

But Jesus does not say, "Forgive us *on the grounds* of the fact that we forgive our debts" but "forgive us *as we also* have forgiven." Here is one of the signs that we belong to God, that He is our Father, that His Son is our Savior and Lord, that His Spirit lives in us. These words, "as we also have forgiven," are the cry of the children telling the Father that they are on His side, that they belong to Him, that they want to be more like Him in purity and righteousness. It is one of the signs that we are among those who have already been forgiven in terms of justification but who also need daily forgiveness in terms of peace and assurance, the sense of the Father's "Well done," and who desire to "go and sin no more."

Those who never forgive, on the other hand, have never understood God or themselves. Leon Morris in his Matthew commentary quotes a fellow writer: "If anyone says 'I'll never forgive you!' that person 'is not penitentially aware of his sins, but only vengefully aware of another man's sins.'"[3] Remember Jesus' parable about the steward who would not forgive his underling even though his master had forgiven him a far greater debt (see Matthew 18:21–35)?

The spur that makes you love much is the sense that you have been loved much. But if your heart is not open to pour out love, it is simply not open for God to pour in love. Let God your Father, in the same act of pouring His love *into* your heart, pour His love *through* your heart into other hearts. And let those hearts include those who might have expected no love from you whom they injured, in order that they may hope for love and forgiveness from God whom they have long opposed.

But if we see sin here in the prayer not as the guilt that damns but as the sin that spoils communion with God, then it further holds true that full and free fellowship with God will not be enjoyed by the Christian believer until he or she seriously and deliberately and openly forgives those who have sinned against him or her. That is not an easy work—but it does bring great freedom, great reward, great demonstrations of love from a heavenly Father who is growing His children into the likeness of Christ Jesus, who is Himself the likeness of God—the God who gives, and forgives, every day of our lives.

NOTES

1. John Stott, *The Cross of Christ* (Downers Grove, Ill.: InterVarsity, 1986), 88–89.

2. Ibid., 89.

3. G. A. Buttrick as quoted in Leon Morris, *The Gospel According to Matthew* (Grand Rapids: Eerdmans, 1992), 147.

Chapter Thirty-Three

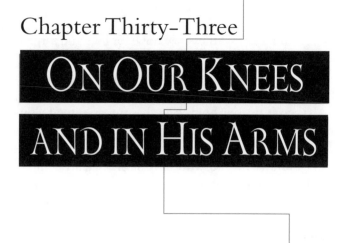

ON OUR KNEES
AND IN HIS ARMS

*D*r. Thomas Barnardo was a generous philanthropist in Victorian England who opened many orphanages. He once told of how a dirty, ragged urchin approached him nervously in the street one day, asking to be taken into one of Barnardo's homes. "I know nothing about you, my lad," said the doctor. "What have you in the way of recommendation?"

"Please sir, I thought these would be enough," murmured the little chap, pointing to his rags. Dr. Barnardo gathered him up in his arms and took him in.

Jesus offers Himself to sinners; others need not apply. "I have not come to call the righteous but sinners" to repentance, He once explained (Matthew 9:13). He calls us as we are, that He might one day make us as we should be. He calls us to come in our rags, with our failures, whispering to Him the things we can tell to no one else. And He takes us in, not as orphans but as dearly loved children. And while repentance has to be renewed every day (for we are daily sinners), His forgiveness, cleansing, and renewing also are available every day.

Let us look more closely now at these themes of repentance, faith, and forgiveness.

The call of God in the gospel is to *repentance* for sin and *faith* in Jesus Christ as Savior and Lord (see Acts 2:38; 17:30). Repentance is quite simply turning to God in sorrow and self-giving. It is not mere regret; feeling sorry that you have committed a sin is not repenting of sin. To reduce repentance to a mood is to lose sight of its life-changing character. Repentance is a change of mind issuing from a change of heart and leading to a change of life. It is a turning toward the light with all that that implies for the creeping things of darkness: the pride, jealousy, and lust that lurk and lodge in dark corners of all our hearts. It is a change of thought and purpose in which a radically new assessment of life is made, with a full and sincere purpose to live to God and walk in His ways. It does not end at conversion but continues and is renewed throughout life.

We can see from this that true repentance is no casual or easy thing. Yet where God is at work, a spirit of humility and sorrow for sin rises within us. Indeed, repentance is God's gift before it is His demand, and we should go to God for it even when we feel we cannot go to God *with* it. God starts where we are and helps us with the first and most tentative steps.

Repentance involves confession, and confession is the acknowledging of our sin, our fault, our debt before God. This is not easy since we are prone to excuse ourselves and to blame others. But we shall not find the relief we most need and which God offers unless we take responsibility for our wrongdoings. We hear a lot these days about "self-discovery," "self-understanding," and "self-affirmation." But we never truly discover ourselves by disguising ourselves. Jesus faces us with our sin, our guilt, our need of Him. Yet in doing so He does not rubbish us; He gives us value! He is saying in effect, "Because you matter so much to me, I am going to deal with you in grace and truth. I am going to accuse you and acquit you; to uncover your filthiness and wash you clean; to turn you from your rebel ways and reconcile you to Myself forever."

This work of personal salvation can never be earned. It can only be received as a gift. The earning has been done by Christ Jesus. We have only to receive Him and what He has done for us in repentance and faith. He is our righteousness, "a righteousness from God" which is gained, not by good works in any degree, but "by faith from first to last" (Romans 1:17). This alone is a righteousness that will survive the uncompromising judgments of God in the Day of Judgment. "Therefore, since we have been justified through faith, we have peace with God through our Lord Jesus Christ, through whom we have gained access by faith into this grace in which we now stand. And we rejoice in the hope of the glory of God" (Romans 5:1–2).

This "faith," so crucial to the personal application of redemption, is not a merely human characteristic. Like repentance (which is its first expression), it is a gift from God (see Ephesians 2:8). Nor is it a synonym for credibility or superstition. Faith is basically a reasonable trust, casting oneself wholly upon Jesus as Savior and Lord based upon what He has done for our salvation; it is coming to Him who will not drive us away (see John 6:37) and surrendering to Him in love and self-giving.

But this trust involves the recognition of our own need and utter insufficiency—and the inadequacy of any other help. As John Calvin has put it: "Faith is nothing more than the empty hand of the beggar receiving the bounty of a giving God." In this there must be the recognition of our sins and the renunciation of self-righteousness.

The result of all this—the cancellation of debts, the lifting of burdens, the forgiveness of sins—will affect more lives than our own. If we know how much we are forgiven, then we shall be readier to forgive others. If we know we are loved—by God and to the utmost—then we shall have a power to love that goes beyond any natural inclination or moralizing. If the joy of our salvation fills us, it will overflow to others also (see Mark 5:19–20).

Chapter Thirty-Four

GOD'S

EXAMPLE

The forgiveness of God is so complete that writers of Scripture ransack their language for symbols strong enough and metaphors forceful enough to describe it. Micah cries:

> Who is a God like you, who pardons sin and forgives the transgression of the remnant of his inheritance? You do not stay angry forever but delight to show mercy. You will again have compassion on us; you will tread our sins underfoot and hurl all our iniquities into the depths of the sea. (7:18–19)

One of the most joyful psalms has this as its center:

> He does not treat us as our sins deserve or repay us according to our iniquities. For as high as the heavens are above the earth, so great is his love for those who fear him; as far as the east is from the west, so far has he removed our transgressions from us. (103:10–12)

Perhaps the most striking expression depicting the complete forgiveness of God is the image of God forgetting. Think of that! The power of the divine memory, like the power of the divine mind and will, is infinite. As a shepherd counts his sheep, so Yahweh counts the number of the stars "and calls them each by name" (Psalm 147:4). Every atom and cell is held in being by Him, every word is weighed and every thought laid bare; His omniscience is total. Yet He says through Jeremiah that a new day is approaching and a new covenant is going to come into operation: "I will forgive their wickedness and will remember their sins no more" (Jeremiah 31:34).

"No power on earth," writes John White, "can touch pardon. Atomic power can vaporize a city. It can raise a mushroom cloud miles into the sky. But it can neither soften a hardened heart, straighten the shoulders of a discouraged person nor break the power of sin."[1]

We are among those whose hearts have been softened, whose shoulders have often been straightened, who have been given fresh courage and purpose in our lives because we have found forgiveness in God and received pardon, ungrudging and unlimited. God, whose Son Jesus taught us to forgive "seventy times seven," is as good as His word—except that He has never counted! Someone once said, "When we go to our Father grieving and anxious, confessing 'Father, I've done it again,' He replies, 'What do you mean "again"?'" He forgives *and forgets.* He does not bind us to our past.

That is what guilt does: it binds us to our sin, to an unforgiven past. We have a powerful illustration of that in the story of Joseph and his brothers in the Old Testament book of Genesis. At the climax of the story Joseph, now chief minister in Egypt, keeps his identity a secret from the brothers who had wronged him. Pretending to believe they are spies, Joseph continues to keep one of them prisoner while the others went back to Canaan for the younger brother, Benjamin. We read: "They said to one another, 'Surely we are being punished because of our brother. We saw how distressed he was when he pleaded with us for his life, but we would not listen; that's why this distress has come upon us.'" (Genesis 42:21). You see the point? They are still loaded with the guilt of their sin committed years before; consequently, when calamity comes they immediately see it as retribution for their wrongdoing (42:22, 28; 44:16). They are chained to their past, and no power can dissolve those chains.

No power, that is, except the power of forgiveness. Joseph's tears dissolve their chains; his love, his forgiveness, and his faith in God finally and definitively free them from their past and free them for a new future.

Here is a lesson for us all from Joseph's brethren. The past is not easily left behind. It has ongoing effects. It has built and shaped the present. We are just not strong enough to deal with the past and reshape the present. Like a once-supple sapling that has become a gnarled, unbending tree, we find our spirits stubborn, our passions too strong for us, or our apathy too paralyzing. We need a power that can forgive us completely and change us fundamentally.

It is confession and the prayer for forgiveness that open up the heart to the surge of love that comes from the Father-heart of God and beats against the doors and windows of a life, seeking entry. And when it gains it, the rush of cleansing that comes in clears us of the rubbish of years. But there can be no forgiveness where there is no repentance, no cleansing where the heart is sullen and sealed. Then our sins only accumulate; we stagger under a growing load of unconfessed wrongdoing; we hide it and absorb its pollution instead of washing it away. We justify ourselves and take shelter in the lie, and this lie becomes part of us and we of it, and there is no shelter.

Where then is the heart set free? Where is repentance to be found and the grace to pray in faith "Father ... forgive"? Not from ourselves but from God, and not from God in the skies but God on the cross; not from God reigning in glory but from God suffering at our hands and forgiving: "When they came to the place called the Skull, there they crucified him. . . . Jesus said, 'Father, forgive them, for they do not know what they are doing'" (Luke 23:33–34).

We do not have to look very far to see who needs forgiveness most, and we do not have to look very far to see where forgiveness may be found. Here, at the cross, hearing such words of love to us even as our sins nail Him there; here, if anywhere, we can confess our sins and seek forgiveness. Here, pride is sapped of its strength and cynicism forgets its lines. Here, God says the words for us and takes the blame for us: "the punishment that brought us peace was upon him" (Isaiah 53:5). It was because He "bore the sin of many, and made intercession for the transgressors" that we can pray, "Forgive us our debts for Jesus' sake" (Isaiah 53:12).

NOTE

1. John White, *The Race* (Downers Grove, Ill.: InterVarsity, 1984), 157.

Chapter Thirty-Five

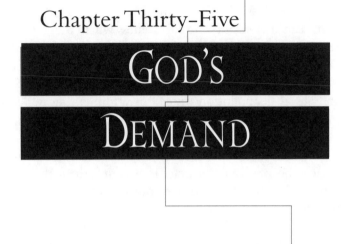

GOD'S

DEMAND

When God forgives us our sins against Him, the first thing He asks us to do is to *forgive others their sins against us.* This is a main part of love, and Jesus said, "Love each other as I have loved you" (John 15:12).

Love is the masterwork that God does at the center of the believer's life. Here, settled in one disposition of the heart, in one overriding attitude, in one ruling power, is the imitation of Christ and the likeness of God. In this the image is restored more than in anything else.

So vital is love that it forms an eleventh commandment given by Jesus (see John 13:34–35), which sums up and embraces all the others. To love God and your neighbor as yourself is the foundation of new life that lives not only by the new commandment but in the power of Him who gave it. For you cannot be legalistic here, even though love is the fulfilling of the law. And you cannot love nominally, any more than you can breathe only on special occasions. As John writes:

> Dear friends, let us love one another, for love comes from God. Everyone who loves has been born of God and knows God. Whoever does not love does not know God, because God is love.... Whoever loves God must also love his brother. (1 John 4:7–8, 21)

However, this does not mean that love is effortless for us. We are not yet in heaven and there are contradictory forces within us as well as around us (see Galatians 5:17). We have the Spirit within us, planting and nurturing His fruit of love, joy, peace, patience, etc. But we still need the command to "keep in step with the Spirit" (Galatians 5:22, 25).

The apostle Paul works this out directly in terms of forgiveness and peace in the churches when he writes to the Colossian Christians: "Therefore, as God's chosen people, holy and dearly loved, clothe yourselves with compassion, kindness, humility, gentleness and patience. Bear with each other and forgive whatever grievances you may have against one another. Forgive as the Lord forgave you" (3:12–13).

We do not find this an easy thing to do. One woman went away deeply convicted after the preacher had spoken on this subject. The next day, when people were being asked to say ways in which they had been blessed, she said, "Last night, when I got home I asked the Lord to help me to throw away my 'despisory.'" She went on to say that she had realized that she kept something like a card index system at the back of her mind of all the things that people had done against her and for which she despised them.[1]

No doubt "forgive and forget" may be easy enough

when the injury is small and the attitude carefree. But when the injury is great or the sense of sin profound, there, in the moment of recoil, to embrace, to turn cursing into blessing, and to seek the sinner behind and beyond the sin, there the victory is profound and the cost of it great. As Simon Tugwell puts it, "Forgiveness is not something for nice people with weak stomachs!"[2]

I agree with those who say this is often a slow process and one that has to be repeated. McClung writes wisely:

> Forgiveness is often a process and not a once only act. We keep on forgiving until the pain goes away. The deeper the wound the greater the forgiveness needed. Just as a doctor has to keep a physical wound in our bodies clean from infection so that this wound can heal properly so we must keep our emotional wounds clean of bitterness so they can heal. Forgiveness keeps the wounds clean. Whenever you think of a particular person and feel hurt, forgive them. Just tell the Lord that you forgive that person and that you choose to love them with God's love. Receive his love for them by faith, keep doing that every time you think of the person, until you feel God's love released in your heart for them.[3]

Rita Nightingale, falsely imprisoned in Thailand on a charge of smuggling heroin, writes of her attempts to forgive:

> It was a slow and painful progression. Each person had to be prayed over, agonised over and forgiven. When I thought I had really forgiven somebody I would find myself resenting them two or three days later and have to forgive them all over again. It was only as I looked back, as the days became weeks and the weeks months, that I saw

my attitudes were changing. I was learning how to for-give.[4]

Here is the victory of faith, the triumph of love, the signature of God on our lives.

There is one person who never forgives because he never loves. That person is Satan. The word *Satan* means *adversary,* and he is called "the accuser of our brothers" (Revelation 12:10). Where he meets malice, he rein-forces it; where he meets goodness, he holds it in con-tempt; where he meets failure and sin in Christian lives, he raises around them a storm of reproach and digs at their feet a pit of despair. He first tempts people into sin and then accuses them of sin. This is especially true of his dealings with God's people. (See, for example, Job 1:9–11; Zechariah 3:1–5.)

And Satan wants us to act similarly when people have sinned against us—people whom we are tempted (in turn) to hate or despise or resent. This brings us to a point of decision. When others have taken advantage of us, or let us down, or spoken ill of us, we have a choice which to us should be no choice at all. I once heard Elisa-beth Elliott say on forgiveness: "You can either stand with Satan against that person or you can stand with Christ for them."

In at least four ways, our faith compels us to forgive others. First, *we are never more like God than when we forgive.* God Himself delights in mercy and loves to forgive. When He revealed Himself in His glory to Moses, God described the center of His glory this way: "The Lord, the Lord, the compassionate and gracious God, slow to anger, abounding in love and faithfulness, maintaining love to thousands, and forgiving wickedness, rebellion and sin" (Exodus 34:6–7).

While He also warns the impenitent that "he does not leave the guilty unpunished," yet judgment is His "strange work," His "alien task" (Exodus 34:7; Isaiah 28:21). He delights in mercy but grieves in judgment (see Micah 7:18; Luke 19:41–44).

It is our duty to forgive because it is God's command and because we ourselves have been forgiven, but it is also our privilege because it is God-like to forgive (see Psalm 86:5). Alas, we would often prefer to be like God in judgment than to be like Him in mercy; more aware of others' sins than our own, and always ready to qualify God's commands with exceptions or to say, "That's enough," when we've only just begun to obey.

Second, *in forgiving others we delight God*. Many have felt the love and joy and peace of God flood their heart as they forgave, especially when that forgiveness was a hard and painful work, as it sometimes is. Nothing pleases the heart of God like mercy, forgiveness, and love. Here He meets the beauty of His own image in us; here He meets the likeness of the Son He loves who prayed for His enemies. Here also those around us meet with the sign of the future in the present, the promise of a new earth where love will face no contradiction.

Even where your forgiveness has met with a poor response from your fellow human beings, get on your knees in a quiet place and let your Father embrace you and encourage you. Christ often whispers His "Well done, good and faithful servant" *before* the final day!

Third, *our disposition is to forgive*. It may be a struggle at times, but it is not only a struggle. The Christian heart is already the place wherein the Holy Spirit makes His dwelling (note Ephesians 2:22). There is a readiness to love and to forgive and to be reconciled to others. Anger and bitterness are not foods we can thrive on, and we can never enjoy the aftertaste of revenge. We have learned a better way of living, for God has changed our hearts and now we are different in action and reaction. We are fools to ourselves when we act as the world expects, for we are acting out of character and distancing ourselves from the God in whom we delight.

It is when we turn the sinful standards of the world on their heads and respond to our Father's very different rules that we astonish the world and perhaps seed hope in hearts long hardened and cynical.

Fourth, *we have encouragement to forgive in every direction.* The forgiving heart is the one that has found and entered upon a great freedom. The forgiving heart has no excuse not to forgive; there can be no refuge for bitterness in its wide landscape (see Matthew 18:21–34). *When we look back* at our own sins and failures, our past ingratitude and present weakness, we should not be inclined to keep alive our own little resentments but when we see how much we have been forgiven and how much we are loved, we may well entertain and cultivate a generous spirit toward others. When we look up to a Christ praying for us (see Hebrews 7:25) and meet His prayers with our own to be more like Him, we may well exchange resentments for prayers and pray for those who use us badly, just as He said when He was here on earth (see Matthew 5:44). *When we look forward* to our eternal future of joy and glory and dare to contemplate the everlasting fate of those who ill-use God more than they ill-use us, we can soon feel pity more than resentment and be ready to lighten their load a little, removing our recriminations at least.

Perhaps the greatest encouragement is the possibility that our love in return for hatred will become the channel of a greater love and an irresistible grace. Such love can capture and rescue those we forgive from an eternal exclusion and bring them to the Father's home (see Luke 15:18–24).

NOTES

1. Marion Ashton, *Growing into Wholeness* (Eastbourne, England: Kingsway, 1985), 42.
2. Simon Tugwell, *Prayer* (Dublin: Veritas, 1974), 82.
3. Floyd McClung, *The Father Heart of God* (Eastbourne, England: Kingsway, 1985), 93.
4. Rita Nightingale, *Freed for Life* (Basingstoke, England: Marshall Pickering, 1982), 176.

Part Five

"AND LEAD US NOT
INTO TEMPTATION,
BUT DELIVER US
FROM THE EVIL ONE"

Chapter Thirty-Six

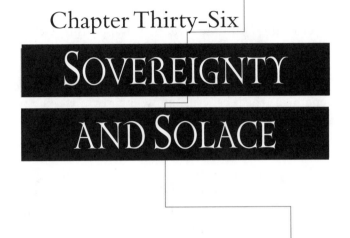

SOVEREIGNTY
AND SOLACE

*A*nd lead us not into temptation but deliver us from the Evil One." In the original languages in which the Bible is written, the same word is used for both *testing* and *tempting.* God is often said to test His people to try to demonstrate the genuineness of their loyalty to Him. This is testing with a good motive. On the other hand, Satan too is said to test the people of God—but with the desire to undermine their faith and destroy their witness, and so bring disgrace to the cause of God or the name of Christ. This is usually what we call temptation. Sometimes in the same event or life experience both God and Satan are at work in different ways for different purposes: God testing, encouraging, strengthening for victory over temptation; Satan pressuring, seducing, weakening if he can, aiming at our defeat and downfall.

This part of the Lord's Prayer, therefore, is a plea by Christians that they might not be led into such over-whelming temptation that they would fall before the power of the Evil One. The prayer appeals to God to deliver from the temptation and from the devil who uses it.

In other words, it is a prayer for protection and strength, in which believers know their own weaknesses and vulnerabilities and confess their daily, hourly need of God's grace and care.

Has God got anything to do with temptation in our lives? The surprising but also comforting answer of Scripture is yes. Of course it's true that God tempts no one in the way that Satan does, and we cannot blame God when we fail in testing times or situations. As James says, we have to accept responsibility for what we do: "When tempted, no one should say, 'God is tempting me.' For God cannot be tempted by evil, nor does he tempt anyone; but each one is tempted when, by his [or her] own evil desire, he is dragged away and enticed" (James 1:13–14).

Yet the Scriptures also make it quite clear that God has an overall sovereignty in life that never leaves Him on the sidelines. He is at the heart of every event and experience of our lives, even of suffering, when He suffers with us, and of temptation, when He stays close to us. And in His time He delivers us from evil.

There is a sense in which God does indeed lead His people into testing situations where they will be tempted. We have a very clear instance of that in the life of Christ. After the account of Jesus' baptism we read: "Then Jesus was led by the Spirit into the desert to be tempted by the devil" (Matthew 4:1).

Isn't it important for us to know this—that in the *tests* of life and at the points of great *pressure* and *tempta-*

tion God is in control, that He will not let us be tempted above our strength, and that He will lead us out into victory and freedom?

But why, you may ask, does God allow it all in the first place? Are we just bit players in the cast of some cosmic pantomime without real meaning or value except to some overworked angels who need to watch a good soap opera?

No, life is for real, and the Bible deals with the real world. It gives us thoughtful and weighty reasons why God allows His people to go through hard times of assault, of suffering and setback, and of temptation. They are not simple answers to complex issues, but they are real ingredients, crucial elements in the spiritual warfare. They comfort us and they strengthen us.

Sometimes God allows us to be tested to show His own commitment and keeping power in our lives. And so the psalmist often celebrates God as his refuge and fortress, his shield and protector (for example, Psalms 3–7).

Sometimes He allows us to be tested to show the truth and quality of His grace in us and our faith in Him and to enable us to reassure others (see Job 1:1, 8, 21; 2 Corinthians 1:4). Who would have heard of Job or been helped by his story if Job had not suffered at Satan's hands?

Sometimes God uses such times and even our falls to humble us and warn others, even as He humbled the overconfident Peter, who caved in to fear and denied his Lord (see Luke 22:31–61; 1 Peter 5:5–6).

Sometimes God does it to make us more understanding toward others—and more approachable, too. Paul writes: "Brothers, if someone is caught in a sin, you who are spiritual should restore him gently. But watch yourself, or you also may be tempted" (Galatians 6:1).

It may seem odd to say it, but sometimes God can even use temptation to save us from sin. Strong temptations sometimes frighten us, showing us what we could be or do without God's power and protection. And so we become more wary of situations we should avoid in the future. Often we would sin more if we were tempted less!

One thing we can be sure of: God may bring us into testing times and hard conflict, but He will always be with us there. He may lead us into temptation, but He will never leave us in temptation, and He will in His own time deliver us out of our trial. "Fear not," God assures us, "for I have redeemed you; I have summoned you by name; you are mine" (Isaiah 43:1).

Chapter Thirty-Seven

TEMPTATION

AS TESTING

*C*olored water can look like wine until you drink it. A car can look sound enough until you drive it. People can seem pleasant and unselfish or stable and helpful until you get to know them or need them. So also, people can have the name of *Christian* without any personal experience of Christ's love and power, without a new heart and a new inner principle of godliness (see Jeremiah 31:33).

Even in the Old Testament period God taught the difference between being *nominally* in His covenant and belonging *personally* to Him. So again and again we read that God tests His own people, Israel, to "see" (really to show) whether they will be true to their place in the covenant. He tested Abraham to show the supreme quality of his faith (see Genesis 22:1–2). He tested Israel in the wilderness to show His own faithfulness and to bring to light both their loyalty and their unfaithfulness (see Deuteronomy 8:1–5, 16–18). He tested the nation in Canaan by keeping them in proximity to alternative religions and lifestyles with the command to be separate as His holy people (see Judges 2:20–23).

Notice how God is said to test His own people, not the nations around them. They do not belong to Him, but Israel does (see Amos 3:2). Similarly, Christians need to understand that such testing in our own lives is not the mark of His wrath but the mark of His love. Testing is not the evidence of His abandonment but the sign of our sonship and daughterhood and His commitment to us. To the nominal believer the test will expose hypocrisy, but to the true believer it acts as a discipline to refine and mature. So the psalmist could say after a testing time: "Before I was afflicted I went astray, but now I obey your word" and "It was good for me to be afflicted so that I might learn your decrees" (Psalm 119: 67, 71). The experience has made the psalmist value God more than ever: "The law from your mouth is more precious to me than thousands of pieces of silver and gold" (Psalm 119: 72).

Times of *persecution for our faith* are outstanding times of testing when stern realities are faced, priorities set at all costs, and personal weaknesses, such as fear, doubt, and selfishness, are faced and dealt with as never before. In a prayer letter during the communist ascendancy a few years back, a Russian believer wrote:

> My first fifteen-day sentence taught me a great deal about myself. In such a situation you see your good and bad points very clearly. You find out where your weaknesses are. Persecution can be compared to a photographic developer. When the film is immersed in the developer, an image appears. When a Christian encounters persecution, his character becomes evident. Our church quickly learned who was ready for persecution and who wasn't.

A wise old man once said to a young Chinese Christian: "A man's faith is like a teabag. It's only in hot water that it shows its true color!" This is a consistent New Testament perspective on times of trial and loss for Christ's cause (for example, 1 Peter 1:6–9). Often the tests consist of *prolonged trials* that "stretch" us. We recognize that we are not immune from the ills and pressures of life; we are prepared to take our share of suffering like good soldiers of Christ (see 2 Timothy 2:3), but then we discover that our share is larger than we expected, the test is greater, the trial longer, the expectation on God's part greater, and we begin to protest. "That's enough now, Lord," we say. "I've learned the lesson. I've got the message. I'm sure I'm better equipped to help others and testify to your all-sufficiency; please stop now!"

But God doesn't stop—the pressures and demands increase, and we remind God that He has promised not to try us above our strength. But He says we've more strength than we know. After a while, we protest that we're at our last gasp—but He simply replies, "Oh no, you've got a few more gasps in you yet." And we always have. And somehow we not only survive but come out conquerors, though we might scarcely know it.

Oswald Chambers has somewhere put it memorably:

A saint's life is in the hands of God like a bow and arrow in the hands of the maker. God is aiming at something the saint cannot see and He stretches and strains and every now and again the saint says "I cannot stand any more". God does not heed but goes on stretching till His purpose is in sight. Then He lets fly. Trust yourself in God's hands.

Often the test consists of *great loss:* the onset of a progressive disease that wastes the muscles or takes the memory, or a terminal cancer in a loved one, or a bereavement where our "Isaac" has to be given up to God. At such times faith may come near to breaking point. "Where was God when my son died?" cried a mother in despair to her pastor. "Where He was when His own Son died," was the quiet reply.

For us all and in all the changing scenes of life, He who loves us and is our helper is on the throne *and* in the situation, suffering with us but also leading us to His glory where every tear will be wiped away by our Father in person (Revelation 21:4). God is with us in the darkest times, and Christ will meet us in these times, placing them among our profoundest spiritual experiences. Meantime, sufferings remain and are a test for us all at some time or other. And it is a sobering fact that troubles will usually drive the nominal believer *from* God and the true believer *to* God.

Sometimes the greatest test in a believer's life may be in prosperity, success, even riches. I have known people who were doing well until these things came and spoiled them! They became proud and overbearing in success or foolishly chose the toys of life when rich and missed opportunities to do serious good.

Sometimes God's best decision is to say no to our requests, to lead us away from the goals we set ourselves, even to disappoint our expectations—and all in answer to our daily prayer, "Lead us not into temptation." We do well to make our goal the *character* that is the priority of the wise man in Proverbs 30:7–9. He knew that temptation can take many forms and he knew his vulnerability on more than one side; so he asks for "neither poverty nor riches, but ... only my daily bread."

At first it may seem strange, in the light of all this, that we should be told to pray that God will not test us, when it is sometimes His way to do so (see James 1:2–4). But the sense of the petition may well be "Do not test us beyond our strength," and it may be so here as a way of confessing to our Father that, in a world of fierce conflict and many dangers, we feel very vulnerable and ill equipped, and feel too the poverty of our faith and love. This is our way of leaning on "the everlasting arms."

Chapter Thirty-Eight

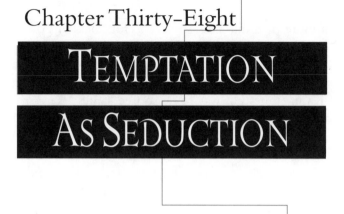

TEMPTATION

AS SEDUCTION

$\mathcal{S}$atan—the Evil One—now why bring him into this? Who needs an outdated mythology to help maintain a modern morality? Who really needs this part of the prayer? Well, I do for one and you do for another. A prayer against temptation that did not include the tempter would be shortsighted, to say the least, and probably short-lived too. Nothing guarantees defeat more than underestimating the enemy, and a Satan relegated to fairyland is an adversary underestimated with a vengeance.

Satan, the great deceiver, can use temptation as seduction. Of course, we must first accept that a personal devil and demons exist in this modern world. Some question that: "Is such a belief not primitive in the extreme? Are such concepts relevant or even coherent to men and women in our society?" However, the Christian believer must not be bullied into silence by incredulity touched with scorn.

Those who dismiss this belief usually dismiss not only Satan but God, not only the demonic but the whole realm of the supernatural. Indeed, that is their problem: They see this world and the physical universe as a closed system where everything can be adequately explained in purely natural terms. They have no room in their world-view for Christian belief as a whole or for this as a part of the Christian's worldview. They have no room for God, for Jesus Christ as the Son God sent into the world, for the need of salvation or the good news that men and women can be reconciled to God through Jesus Christ.

They are at a polar extreme from their ancestors, who went in dread of evil spirits every day, who saw them behind every tree and in every event, and who sought to charm or bribe them lest they were possessed or slain by them. These descendants have, if I might change the image, moved from the tropics to the ice cap, from a world overpeopled with spirits to a bleak and icy world where humanity lives alone, dug in against the cold of its own hopelessness, without God or a gospel that rises above death and opens a way beyond it.

C. S. Lewis wrote:

> There are two equal and opposite errors into which our race can fall, about the devils. One is to disbelieve in their existence. The other is to believe and to feel an excessive and unhealthy interest in them. They themselves are equally pleased by both errors and hail a materialist or a magician with the same delight.[1]

Further, we ignore Scripture if we ignore this matter. We do not find in Scripture either "an excessive and unhealthy interest" in or an unreal avoidance of the matter. The Old Testament tells us of the temptation of Eve, the testing of Job, and the accusation of Joshua, all by

Satan, and it recognizes the reality of demonic presence and activity in the world (for example, 1 Samuel 16:15–23; 1 Kings 22:21–23), especially, in the worship of false gods. Jesus clearly believed in the existence of Satan as a personal and distinct being and told His followers of one encounter of particular force that He experienced after His baptism.

In the Gospels we find many explicit references to Satan and his power in the earth, but also the clear announcement that the kingdom of God has come in with Jesus' ministry, and that, as light drives darkness back, so Christ in His kingdom activity will rob Satan of his possessions, bringing men and women throughout the earth to freedom. While on earth Jesus' deliverance from the Evil One took various forms, ranging from exorcism through certain healings and on to the preaching of the gospel.

Today as ever, and in our land as in any, Satan continues his work, encouraging rebellion against God, blinding men and women to the truth of the gospel, lulling some to sleep and engulfing others in violence (see 1 John 5:19; 1 Peter 5:8–9). So the cry goes up from believers, who are not exempt from Satan's cunning, deceit, and malice: "Deliver us from the Evil One."

Such a prayer, however, need not be the dying gasp of a drowning man but the daily recognition that "the reason the Son of God appeared was to destroy the works of the devil"(1 John 3:8 RSV). In that confidence we may face temptation and opposition and all danger. We do not know ourselves or our situation if we imagine that we do not need this prayer or its warning.

We like to think that we are very reasonable, sensible, self-controlled and self-determining beings. Yet for all this we are complex and contradictory creatures. Our attitudes are often formed and affected subconsciously, by forces and influences of which we are only dimly aware. Our behavior is much affected by external pressures, influences, and limitations, and many forces in society "pull our strings." We are neither as free nor as fine as we like to think. D. M. Lloyd-Jones wrote:

> The fatal mistake made constantly about man is to regard him only as a mind or an intellect; and therefore the whole basis of secular teaching is that all you need to do is to tell men about the evil nature of certain things.... Conversely, if you tell them to do certain things because they are right and good and true and noble, they will jump at them and do them. What ignorance of human nature! ... They will not see that man in the main is irrational ... a kind of iceberg—two-thirds out of sight in the depth, in the darkness ... man is not governed by His mind, His intellect, His understanding, but by His desires, impulses, and instincts, by what the psychologists call "drives."[2]

And it is here in particular that Satan is very active, for evil is in its own nature very irrational, incoherent, inconsistent, and elusive. Reason is for Satan a weapon, a means to an end, a way to manipulate a situation. But it is also dispensable, and it can easily be circumvented. Often we ourselves use our intellects in the service of our prejudices, our passions, and our lusts, which have been encouraged or enticed by Satan. Michael Green cited a striking example of this:

> Aldous Huxley ... admits with delightful candour that he was unwilling to commit himself to the demands of Christian discipleship. In a fascinating passage in *Ends and*

Means he writes: "I had motives for not wanting the world to have a meaning; consequently assumed that it had none, and was able without any difficulty to find satisfying reasons for this assumption.... For myself, the philosophy of meaninglessness was essentially an instrument of liberation, sexual and political."[3]

It is clear from Scripture that Satan's great hatred is for God; his great desire is to oppose, dishonor, and defeat God. Having been cast from heaven, he continues that warfare on earth, seeking the corruption and destruction of the unique race God made to share His eternity. In particular, he seeks to corrupt, divert, or destroy the church of God on earth, the one agency that exists to reclaim a lost world and to save men and women. His malice and subtlety are particularly directed against the people of God in all ages. Because of that he is called "the accuser of the brethren"—though I hasten to add that he is not gender-specific in his accusations! He is out to accuse us before God and other people, to mock God and to discredit us. He even accuses us to ourselves: He takes away shame when he tempts us and then piles it on when we give in, so that we are ashamed even to come to God for forgiveness.

Let me take you briefly through some of the stages of seduction, the steps of temptation to evil, that Satan employs.

First, he presents the temptation in its most attractive form, however ugly the reality. Like an angler, he presents the bait and hides the hook: he shows us the enjoyment or the profit of the wrongdoing and hides the later guilt and shame and hurt that we shall feel. The only way to be safe here is to keep away from the bait as well as the hook! It may be wrong company, a wrong relationship a wrong book or film, a step in the wrong direction in career advancement. You cannot pray "Lead us not into temptation" if you lead yourself into temptation!

Second, he persuades. After he presents, he persuades. He cannot force you into sin but he can talk you into sin, engaging you in a fascinating conversation on the rights and wrongs of it all. And he is an expert in debate, especially on ethics! He can argue things onto their heads, calling evil good and good evil and supporting it by a series of seemingly watertight arguments. (See Genesis 3:1, 4–5; Isaiah 5:20; Matthew 4:1-11.) He will tell you to be yourself when he is only taking you further and further from your true self. He will talk of self-fulfillment even as he leads you to self-disintegration. He will imply that you can join the rat race without becoming one of the rats. He will persuade you not to be ashamed to sin— only ashamed to repent and return to God.

Third, he persists. One swallow doesn't quench a thirst and one victory doesn't win a war; neither does one self-denying decision for God mean the end of the matter. Ours is a spiritual warfare that lasts as long as life in this battlefield world lasts. Satan has no sense of honor or fair dealing, and he will follow us through a life of service to Christ and into old age, still tempting, persisting, sowing doubts and fears in our weakest, most vulnerable hours.

Hence we see the solemn need for Christians to develop their spiritual life. If there is consistent attack and erosion in one or two sensitive areas in our lives, we must be on guard and daily praying and seeking strength in precisely those areas.

Fourth, he presses upon us. In his famous passage on the

believer taking "the full armor of God" to withstand Satan's attacks, Paul spoke of "the day of evil." Whatever else that "day of evil"(Ephesians 6:13) may mean, it is a fact of Christian experience that you will encounter days of special pressure and significant temptation, when evil comes in like a flood.

At such times our cry to God will be strongest, but so will be His protection if we trust in Him and strive with Him against the pressures of the hour. He has promised He "will not let you be tempted beyond what you can bear. But when you are tempted, he will also provide a way out so that you can stand up under it" (1 Corinthians 10:13). However, it is surprising what we can bear with God's help, and the trial may be both long and hard. Such times are not to be lightly regarded: we cannot say, in foolish, vain confidence, "I'll never fall" or "I can take it." Better to know our own weakness and pray daily: "Lead us not into temptation, but deliver us from the Evil One."

Let Paul's words be our wisdom and our warning: "For our struggle is not against flesh and blood, but against . . . the spiritual forces of evil in the heavenly realms. . . . With this in mind, be alert and always keep on praying for all the saints (Ephesians 6:12, 18). In the next two chapters we will study two common areas of temptation—the intellectual life and the moral life—and two specific temptations within those areas.

NOTES

1. C. S. Lewis, *The Screwtape Letters* (New York: Macmillan, 1961), 3.
2. D. M. Lloyd-Jones, *The Christian Warfare* (Edinburgh: Banner of Truth, 1976), 29.
3. Michael Green, *Running from Reality* (Downers Grove, Ill.: InterVarsity, 1983), 62.

Chapter Thirty-Nine

INTELLECTUAL TEMPTATION: THE TEMPTATION TO DOUBT

Satan's primary and most persistent temptation is toward unbelief and rebellion. There are many turnings from the road of faith, which deviate gradually until we are going in a quite opposite direction. Satan often tempts us not at first to defiance, but to doubts. He tempts us to doubt God's existence on the one hand or God's commitment to us on the other hand, the reality of His threats or the validity of His promises, the wisdom of His laws or the truth of His gospel. Temptation now, as ever, is usually prefaced by, "Did God really say . . . ?" (Genesis 3:1).

Faith always has to deal with doubts, from early youth to late age. Doubt is often waiting round the next corner with the unexpected, or lurking in the undergrowth of a new argument, or curled up in a bad experience, or tracking our footsteps alongside an old problem. Satan never gives up. If he cannot destroy you, he will try to disturb you. And he knows that doubts disturb us deeply; they hurt us precisely in proportion to our love for God, our longing for Him, our surrender to Him. That is why the best of us will be beset with doubts from time to time. A world-famous missionary leader, George Verwer of Operation Mobilization, said recently to our congregation, "I've lived my whole life on the edge of agnosticism. So you people who talk of your doubts all the time, look, any idiot can doubt; faith just costs a little bit more." After thirty years of faithful, fruitful but not peaceful service, he should know!

Hence we all need to learn to handle doubts in a mature, stable way: not pretending, not panicking, and not pitying ourselves into spiritual depression and vulnerability, but coping with the strong winds of temptation and dealing patiently with the grit that gets into the eyes of faith at times so that we cannot see too well for a while. And this means that it is indeed *faith* that must handle doubt: not fear, not an enforced neutrality, not a helpless compliance, but faith.

The way to approach your doubts is first to understand your faith. And when I speak of your faith I mean the faith— the great historic facts and the glorious spiritual realities of the Christian faith. Not, in the first place, your believing, but your beliefs. That way you don't start with the negative and you don't start with yourself! Faith grows strong by looking to God and to what He has done, by listening to God and understanding His will and way.

This was the psalmist's way in Psalm 73. There he tells us he nearly lost his faith when he saw how the godless prosper (vv. 2, 12–13). He felt guilty about this but could not shake it off "till I entered the sanctuary of God; then I understood their final destiny" (v. 17). Before the massive reality of God, the Judge of all the earth, and in the perspective of final judgments and ultimate things, he saw how hollow the pride of the unbelieving was and how foolish he had been to quarrel with God (vv. 18–22). He saw that what mattered supremely in his own experience was that he was loved by God and held in an eternal relationship (vv. 23–26). The rest could wait God's time, God's hour, and God's resolution. So the psalm begins and ends with statements of triumphant and joyful faith: "God is good" and "as for me, it is good to be near God" (vv. 1, 28). This is faith's "bottom line."

We must always be aware that our lives exist, even as Christians, in the world of the Fall. A global catastrophe has distanced our world from God's heaven, wrapping it in silence from the sight or sound of spiritual and supernatural realities. Our world is not normal, and God's dealings with it are not normal. Even with believers, God's dealings are to a very real extent conditioned by sin in the world and in ourselves. Hence while He is the God who speaks, He is often silent (Psalm 28:1); while He is the God who is near, He is often felt as far away (Psalm 22:1–2); and while He is the God of many mercies, "we must go through many hardships to inherit the kingdom of God" (Acts 14:22).

If faith is to cope with the world as it is, we must realize that the world as it is is not the world as it was meant to be. It is a damaged world, and ours is a broken humanity, kept in the mercy of God yet reaping the fruit of man's Fall. God, as Isaiah so beautifully shows in his prophecies (especially chapters 11 and 60–66), has a wonderful future for our world, a future in which it (and we) will be healed and glorious. Yet in the present so many times we have to say, as Isaiah does, "Truly you are a God who hides himself" (45:15).

Doubts come as we look at the shadows, at the apparent absence of God in situations, but faith listens to the promise, looks forward to the reconciliation, and rejoices in the light.

For the New Testament believer, the Christian, much more is clear, for while "the law was given through Moses; grace and truth came through Jesus Christ" (John 1:17). He is the great antidote to doubt, and His stature dwarfs all doubt. So when you are tempted to doubt, start with your objective faith, not your subjective doubts. Is your faith well-founded on the historic reality of Jesus, on the reliability of His claims, and on the coherence of His gospel? The way to approach your doubts is to understand your faith: Is it reasonable, is it well-founded, is it effective? Often Christians know too little about the faith they profess. They carry a Sunday school faith into a university world; they are experts in their field but amateurs in their faith.

And if your faith is intellectually developed *is it put into practice,* is it an active faith? Doubt is only properly dealt with by faith developed in understanding and obedience. Passive intellectual cogitation is not enough. Faith must be put to work; it cannot remain strong and healthy kept only in the inner life.

Second, *we must distinguish between our doubts on the one hand and our attitude toward them on the other.* Christian people are often deeply upset by the presence of doubt. They begin to ask, "If we doubt, does that mean we are not really Christians at all? Does doubting damn us?"

The answer to that last question is probably that one kind of doubting does; another kind does not.

If you prefer doubt to belief, if you hide behind your doubts as convenient excuses to keep you from facing God and His call on your life, if you cherish your doubt and side with it—then you show that you are not, after all, on the side of God, but still running from Him. Your doubt in that case is really unbelief and it is unbelief that damns. The "double-minded man" of James 1:5–8 is not the true believer, faithful but fighting. He is rather the man who still hasn't decided where his loyalty lies; he is "unstable in all he does." His doubt is not a troublesome relic of the old life but a fundamental ambivalence about God.

However, if, quite differently from this, you struggle with doubt in hope and fear, longing to be altogether God's child and hating everything that comes between you and God, including especially doubt and disobedience, then your struggle with doubt is not a sign of unbelief but its opposite. It is a sign of faith. Your very fear is your comfort!

It is not the presence of doubt but the absence of faith that is the damning thing. Faith can and often does coexist with doubt, but it is not equaled by it nor need it be crippled by it. Faith by its very nature is stronger than doubt, as light by its very nature is stronger than darkness. We are "justified by faith," not by the amount of faith but by the truth of faith. If it leads us to Christ as Savior and Lord, it is saving faith, however small and frail it may be. This is because ultimately it is Christ as the object of faith who saves, not faith in itself, and a strong Savior can say to a weak faith, "Daughter, your faith has healed you.

Go in peace and be freed from your suffering" (Mark 5:34).

Third, *we must get our doubts themselves into proper perspective.* When we struggle with doubts, we must not blindly give them a credit they do not deserve. We are inclined to flatter our doubts and to be afraid of them because of a reputation we ourselves have given to them. We often give them a character for honesty and intellectual strength that they do not deserve. Often we are fooled into respecting our doubts more than our beliefs, as if our doubts were free of any prejudice, of anything irrational or even of anything mistaken.

The fact is, of course, that your doubts are no bigger or stronger or more formidable than your own little intellect. They are as susceptible to your very unintellectual sinfulness and weakness and instability as anything else in your life. Often our doubts (which we sometimes run away from instead of facing down) are not nearly as formidable or unanswerable as we think at first. Some small dogs can set up a furious barking as we pass their gate, making us jump nearly out of our skins, but they beat a hasty retreat when we take a step toward them. So it can be with the doubts we fear to voice and examine: they can be toy poodles pretending to be big Alsatians!

What is of supreme importance in this whole matter, whether our doubts are few or many, weak or strong, is what we do with them in relation to Jesus Christ.

Some years ago, a young man from a fine Christian family came to me. He was about to go up to Cambridge to study but knew he was leaving behind a matter which had never been resolved. All his life he had shown great respect for his parents' faith and consistently joined them in church attendance, yet he himself had not made a pro-fession of faith. "You see," he said to me with a slight smile, "I can't shelve my doubts."

"No, but I see that you can shelve your Savior," I replied. He looked startled but interested, and I contin-ued. "You see, something has to be in the center of your life and some things have to be on the shelves—and you've chosen to put Jesus Christ on the shelves. My point is that He ought to be in the center and the doubts on the shelves, but you have exactly reversed that.

"Now I want to ask you whether you really believe that Jesus is small enough to be on the shelf. Personally I think *that* ought to be your biggest doubt, and that you should transfer most of the respect you are giving to your doubts to Him, and that you should put Him in the cen-ter and your doubts on the shelves. Isn't it time to do that?"

I am glad to say that one week later he made an appointment to see me and tell me that Jesus was off the shelf and at the center! You see, it isn't having doubts but what you do with them that matters most.

Chapter Forty

MORAL TEMPTATION: THE TEMPTATIONS OF OUR SEXUALITY

*G*od has made our human race in two genders, male and female. We share His image and dignity, which places us above all other created life-forms in this world (see Genesis 1:27–28). We are made for God and each other and are in various ways incomplete without our fellow human beings (see Genesis 2:18). We are not solitary but social creatures and need each other in different ways and at different levels. We need to belong, both in families and in wider groupings: we need friends and we need families, we need partnerships in our working lives and we need partners in our domestic lives.

The highest form of partnership is an exclusive, lifelong union between husband and wife: a union that restores an ancient oneness (see Genesis 2:22–24) and can make possible again an ancient trust, intimacy, and acceptance: "The man and his wife were both naked, and they felt no shame" (v. 25). We might with justification say that Adam and Eve stood before each other with nothing to hide, open and transparent to one another, mentally and physically. But the text is not to be "spiritualized"; it refers to their sex lives if it refers to anything.

There is a long antisexual tradition in the Christian church, but it is not a biblical one. Genesis tells us that God made us sexual beings from the start. The monastic and ascetic ideals of the early and medieval church could not cope with that. It misread Paul, elevated celibacy above marriage, regarded sexuality as part of the fallenness of human nature, and left a tragic legacy of shame and confusion. As Lewis Smedes put it: "Augustine could not imagine an innocent person in paradise turned on sexually; a sinless Adam could never have been aroused by a pure Eve: Adam and Eve could not have walked with God in the day and made spontaneous love at night. ... This was how Augustine felt about sexuality."[1]

But this is a far cry from the descriptions in Genesis or the Song of Songs or by Jesus or Paul. Sex with all its joys was God's idea before it was ours. Jesus celebrated marriage by His own presence at weddings and taught the basis of gender distinction, the God-givenness of marriage, and the sanctity of sexual union (see Matthew 19:4–6). The apostle Paul was far from the frigid misogynist of popular myth. He understood profoundly the psychology of sex (see 1 Corinthians 6:16), the importance of sex in marriage (see 1 Corinthians 7:3–5), and the uniqueness of sexual union in uniting persons, not only bodies. He even made it an illustration of the perfect union between Christ, the Bridegroom, and the church, His bride.

However, the Bible is a thoroughly realistic book. We are no longer in Eden. Sin has disturbed society in many

ways, including the unique society of husband and wife.
It has brought domination, manipulation, and deceit into
the most sacred of human relationships (see Genesis
3:16), and it has debased the most profound of its intimacies, sexual union. There are, in the New Testament, several lists of human sins and vices. (See, for example, Mark
7:20–23; Galatians 5:19–21; 1 Corinthians 6:9–11.)
From them we learn several important lessons in regard
to our subject, including:

- *Our sexuality is important to God and our misuse of our
  sexuality is a serious sin.* From the prominence sexual
  sins receive in biblical lists—they either head the list
  or occur repeatedly during them—it is clear that the
  sexual drive is both strong and seriously affected by
  the Fall. Our sexuality has become badly distorted
  and is to an extent out of control. Its satisfaction has
  become an end in itself, not an expression of self-
  giving, faithful love or a precious part of the process
  of having children. This matters greatly to God, not
  because sex is wrong or forbidden, but because
  when distorted or misdirected or abused, it
  becomes something else, something without the
  beauty, truth, or meaning of His original gift.
- *Sexual sins exist alongside other equally serious sins.*
  People "clean" of sexual immorality may be cor-
  rupted by greed, distorted with malice, cruel in
  slander, utterly condemned in arrogance. Such people may do as much, or more, harm, yet they often
  look down on those guilty of sexual immorality or
  promiscuity. They may, in the words of the old couplet by English poet Samuel Butler:

> Compound for sins they are inclined to
> By damning those they have no mind to.[2]

The seriousness of other sins, however, does not lessen the seriousness of sexual sin.

- *Sexual misbehavior is an evil that promotes further evil.* Paul in Galatians 5 speaks of "sexual immorality, impurity and debauchery," and later in the list he adds "hatred, discord, jealousy, fits of rage" (vv. 19, 20). And it is a fact of life, as we read in our newspapers every day, that much jealousy, bitterness, discord, and violence grows out of fornication and adultery. No one lives to themselves, and no one sins to themselves alone either. We never know where sin will end. We cannot be permissive in one thing only.

It is against such a background in Scripture that we are able to recognize the powerful forces of moral decay and decadence in our own day, when temptation to sexual sin is more widespread than ever. TV and films, books, and magazines are to a striking degree preoccupied with sex and are providing an increasing amount of sexually explicit material that is turning us into a nation of voyeurs. The privacy of sex is invaded because the sacrosanct nature of sex is discarded. Younger children are bombarded with reports or images of behavior which they cannot emotionally understand, and teenagers have passions excited which they cannot satisfy with marital sex and are increasingly seduced into premarital sex. Parents often feel helpless before outside forces that shape their children's views and expectations, but often do not themselves have a sufficient moral basis for their own moral code.

Churches and Christians are not unaffected by a society where sex is marketed so cleverly and so seductively. Our moral standards have become lower too, in the films we see and the books we read and even the lives we lead, and sometimes our children's standards are lower still. Many who enter the churches today, as new converts to Christ, have said confessions of sexual abuse, promiscuity, pornography, and divorce through unfaithfulness, and sadly not a few Christian lives and their witness over many years are being ruined by surrender to sexual temptations.

In *The Snare,* a perceptive and practical book on sexual temptation, Lois Mowday writes:

> Romans 12:2 says "Do not conform any longer to the pattern of this world but be transformed by the renewing of your mind." It's getting tougher and tougher to have a Romans 12 mind-set when we live in a Romans 1 world: "God . . . gave them over to a depraved mind to do what ought not to be done. They have become fitted with every kind of wickedness, evil, greed and depravity." (Romans 1:28–9)[3]

If we are to be transformed by the renewing of our minds, then those minds will have to be filled with better thoughts, better images, and better standards than we see in the world around. We might do well to place on our TV sets the words of the apostle Paul to a church of young converts who also lived in a permissive society: "Whatever is true, whatever is noble, whatever is right, whatever is pure, whatever is lovely, whatever is admirable

—if anything is excellent or praiseworthy—think about such things. . . . And the God of peace will be with you" (Philippians 4:8–9).

Sexual sin begins in the mind, with a look and a thought that are welcomed and cherished when they ought to be rejected and loathed. People involved in wrong sexual relationships often say and feel that the temptation was too strong for them, that the attraction was just too great, even that the love was too real. But in fact there was a time in its early stages when the temptation could have been dealt with quite easily, when the attraction could have been countered, the occasions of it denied. It is at that much earlier point, when conscious decisions are made in small things, that a line is crossed and a process gets under way that gets out of control. The cry "It's gone too far, the feelings are too strong, I can't help it any more" is not only a cry of helplessness but a confession of guilt—guilt belonging to an earlier point. The critical sin was committed long before the open sin. Mowday argues that "immorality is a process" and warns: "any of us could be in the process right now,"[4] free of open sin, clear of gross sin, but unexpectedly, dangerously, near the top of the slippery slope:

> So, if you think you are standing firm, be careful that you don't fall! No temptation has seized you except what is common to man. And God is faithful; he will not let you be tempted beyond what you can bear. But when you are tempted, he will also provide a way out so that you can stand up under it. (1 Corinthians 10:12–13)

The way out may be the direction in which you look—or stop looking. (Billy Graham said, "You can't help the first look; you can help the second!") The way out may be avoiding company at work or church that part of you enjoys too much. The way out may be an early conversation with your wife or husband, who can help decisively in dealing with unwanted attentions and with early (and still harmless) attractions. The way out may well be a greater care to develop the attractions and intimacies of your own married life. (Read carefully Proverbs 5:18–20; Song of Songs 4:1–15.) But a way out always exists—and at the end of it we will find a wise and good Father who comforts us, encourages us, and leads us on.

NOTES

1. Lewis Smedes, *Sex for Christians* (Grand Rapids: Eerdmans, 1994), 5.
2. Samuel Butler lived from 1612 to 1680. The couplet appears in his epic poem *Hudibras,* part 1:c, l. 213.
3. Lois Mowday, *The Snare* (Colorado Springs: Navpress, 1988), 90.
4. Ibid., 84.

Chapter Forty-One

TARGETS OF TEMPTATION

*W*e are all targets of temptation, yet there are certain times in our lives, and particular situations, in which we can experience very strong assaults from the enemy.

The new Christian is vulnerable in many respects. As a new follower of Christ, your faith is so new, so young, so weak perhaps, that you may be hardly sure that you are a Christian and have real faith. Doubts may come from unexpected directions and the new believer may be unsure how to handle them, thinking that their very presence argues the absence of true faith.

The new Christian may be, as yet, hardly aware of the demands of discipleship or the implications of compromise. It may be a shock and a disappointment to discover that things long cherished may have to be cleared out if his life is to be cleaned up, that lifestyles must change, maybe in dramatic ways, that a comfortable privacy has to be opened up to others as well as to God, that indifference has to give way to concern and to involvements that are sometimes costly. He may be surprised by the enemy into thinking that his new state or delightful Christian experience has put him beyond the reach of temptation. But he will learn that the pendulum of human emotion can swing from the sublime to the sinful in a very short space of time. (See, for instance, Peter's declaration and denial in Matthew 16:16–17 and 22–23.)

The new Christian may be, as yet, unfamiliar with the Christian armory—the weapons of prayer, Scripture, the counsel of older believers, the teaching of experienced preachers, etc. She may repeat in her own Christian life the pattern of Jesus' experience: After His baptism in the Jordan He faced His temptation in the wilderness. So for the new believer all that joy and peace, all the new discoveries of faith in the gospel, all sense of its truth and its relevance, may be challenged in the first weeks. The waters of Jordan soon evaporate in the deserts of Judea; the atmosphere of Sunday can soon be dispersed on Monday. Consequently she must learn to walk by faith, not by feelings, storing up in mind and heart the Word of God, the sure promises of Christ, and the perspectives of Scripture.

If you are a new Christian, you have to meet the demands of the day in prayer and its challenges in the Spirit of Christ. You need to be with other Christians frequently for mutual strengthening and encouragement. And those needs are most urgent in the early days of faith.

The strategic Christian is also a particular target of temptation. You may be a light in a dark place, the only Christian in the family or at work or in a club. Others know you, others watch you; they have a right to expect more of you than they do of others, and they may one day come to you for help they cannot get from others. There are words only you can speak, love only you can give, a gospel only you can share. If Satan can blot your copybook by inconsistencies now, he will. If he can alienate you from others, build up new barriers, sow further misunderstandings, justify and increase prejudice, he will. They do not know it, but you are their only hope under God, and if Satan can blast that to pieces, he will.

You may be a leader of others in your local church or a leader in the making, missionary or evangelist or pastor. If the tempter can get to you, he has won a victory not only in your life but in the lives of many others who look up to you as a model and a guide. Consider the warning of that great Puritan evangelist and theologian of the seventeenth century, Richard Baxter:

> Take heed to yourselves because the tempter will make his first or sharpest onset on you. He bears you the greatest malice who are committed to doing *him* the greatest harm. He knows what a rout he may make among the people if the leaders fall before their eyes.... You will have his most subtle insinuations and incessant solicitations and violent assaults. As wise and learned as you are take heed lest he outwit you. The Devil is a greater scholar than you and a nimbler controversialist ... he will play the juggler with you undiscerned and cheat you of your faith or innocency and you shall not know that you have lost it; nay, he will make you believe it is multiplied or increased when it is lost.[1]

Even *the older Christian* is a particular target of temptation. Sometimes sick and depressed, sometimes lonely and nervous and often assailed by doubts, the older Christian is vulnerable. With seemingly all passion spent, there may be little excitement in the present and some disillusionment with the past. And Satan, "a liar and the father of lies" (John 8:44), will tell you that it was all in vain, all a beautiful dream or a hollow mockery. If ever there was a time to lean your full weight on God, it is now. If ever there was a time to take Jesus Christ at His word ("In my Father's house are many rooms, if it were not so, I would have told you" [John 14:2]), it is now. If ever there was a time to rest on the foundation God has laid, it is now. As one old woman said, "I often tremble on the Rock but the Rock never trembles under me." Nothing can reverse a life entrusted into the hands of Christ and nothing can rob Him of that life, any more than it can rob us of His life. (Indeed He assures us that "no one can snatch them out of my hand" [John 10:28–30].)

The worldly Christian is one person in a category of his own, foolishly making himself a target of temptation, presuming that God will still keep him from sin. But always remember, you cannot pray "Lead us not into temptation" if you lead yourself into temptation. There are books you cannot read, films you cannot see, company you cannot keep, thoughts you cannot entertain if you want to stay safe, away from the slippery slope that leads to the cliff edge. If you know you have a weakness in an area, don't test it—you may be tempting God and delighting Satan.

I often tell the story of a wealthy woman who decided she would hire a chauffeur to drive her about. After receiving several replies to her advertisement, she interviewed each applicant. They all seemed to be satisfactory, but as the interview ended she asked one final question: "Tell me, as a matter of interest, how near to danger could you drive me and still keep me safe?" "Oh madam," said the first easily, "I could drive you to within an inch of danger and you would be safe." The second at his interview replied with even more confidence, "Madam, I could take you to within a hair's breadth of danger and you would be quite safe in my hands." The third candidate for the job, however, looked mystified and rather shocked by the question. "Madam," he responded, "I couldn't answer such a question as that. *I always drive as far from danger as I possibly can.*" He got the job.

That is the only satisfactory way of living this prayer: stay away from temptation, as far away as you possibly can.

For all of us, young and old, new and experienced believers, temptation is a fact of spiritual life which should not take us unawares.

We often become particular targets of temptation *before or after an especially fruitful or decisive work for God.* Christians in leadership, such as preachers, pastors, or evangelists, need to be on their guard at such times. It can lift our spirits and sharpen our awareness to recognize that when we feel particularly embattled and struggling we may be about to enter upon a time of significant advance—and that the enemy knows it! On the other hand, it has been a too-common experience that after a time of spiritual blessing and ministerial fruitfulness we can relax our guard and be overtaken by sudden temptation when we, and others, least expect it. Charles Wesley used to warn about "the swing of the pendulum" in times of revival, and it is a danger in or after any time of high spiritual excitement.

NOTE

1. Richard Baxter, *The Reformed Pastor* (Edinburgh: Banner of Truth, n.d.), ch. 1, sect. 2.

Chapter Forty-Two

CHRIST'S
WORK FOR US

We live in a world blasted by sin and in a life land-mined with temptation. Each of us as a Christian is living his or her own "pilgrim's progress." Will we make it? Will we hold on to the end? If it were left to us, our response to that would hardly be a confident yes. But in fact that "yes" has been sounded for us by a victorious Christ (see John 10:27–28) and a confident apostle (see Philippians 1:6). Our deliverances from sin's powerful attractions and Satan's persuasive temptations are the result of the work of Christ for us and the work of the Holy Spirit in us. In this chapter, we consider Christ's finished work.

First, *we are delivered from evil by the death of Christ for us.* We often hear of the death of our Lord Jesus Christ as delivering us from the penalty of sin, but far less that it has delivered us from the power of sin. And yet this is a clear New Testament emphasis. Thus Paul writes to the Colossians that God "has rescued us from the dominion

of darkness and brought us into the kingdom of the Son
he loves, in whom we have redemption, the forgiveness
of sins" (1:13–14) and to the Galatians that the Lord
Jesus Christ "gave himself for our sins to rescue us from
the present evil age" (1:4).

F. F. Bruce writes on these words: "Paul's 'evil age'
here is an age dominated by an ethically evil power. . . .
Those who accept the gospel are thereby delivered from
the godless *Zeitgeist* (dominating power, moving spirit)."
The atoning death of Christ "delivers them from the
realm where sin is irresistible into the realm where Jesus
himself is Lord."[1]

The same message is repeated in Paul's letter to Titus
where he speaks of the church waiting for the coming of
"our great God and Savior, Jesus Christ, who gave himself for us to redeem us from all wickedness and to purify
for himself a people that are his very own, eager to do
what is good" (2:13–14).

We often use the image of a first-century slave mar-
ket to illustrate the meaning of redemption—deliverance
by the payment of a price, deliverance by purchase. But
in Romans 6 Paul also uses it to illustrate the Christian's
freedom from the tyranny of sin. There, sin is pictured as
a slave owner from whom we have been set free (vv. 14,
17–18, 20), who has no more rights over us and to whom
we have no obligations: "But now that you have been set
free from sin and have become slaves to God, the benefit
you reap leads to holiness, and the result is eternal life.
For the wages of sin is death, but the gift of God is eternal
life in Christ Jesus our Lord" (Romans 6:22–23).

Martin Luther used to tell a quaint story to illustrate
this. When asked how he used to deal with temptation,

he would reply: "Well, when the devil comes knocking at my door and asks, 'Who lives here?' my divine Master the Lord Jesus goes to the door and says, 'Martin Luther used to live here but he has moved out. Now I am the master of the house.'"

Second, *we are delivered from evil by the prayers of Christ for us.* The death of Jesus achieves our salvation, but it's Christ's risen life, power, and prayers that *apply* that salvation. In that respect there is an ongoing and day-by-day deliverance in our lives: a deliverance from Satan, temptation, and sin in particular. Shortly before His passion and after celebrating the Passover, our Lord predicted the denials of Peter, but He also promised his recovery in faith and life: "Simon, Simon, Satan has asked to sift you as wheat. But I have prayed for you, Simon, that your faith may not fail. And when you have turned back, strengthen your brothers" (Luke 22:31).

That the prayer life of Jesus went far beyond His immediate disciples and even His own time on earth is clear from the insights we are given in John 17 (more aptly called "The Lord's Prayer" than this of ours!). There Jesus prays not only for the disciples but also for "those who will believe in me through their message" (v. 20), the "other sheep" which He had spoken of once before (John 10:16), who He would bring into the family and fold of God. They would be under many pressures, from their own families, from their society, and, above all and in all, from Satan: "My prayer is not that you take them out of the world but that you protect them from the evil one" (John 17:15).

The writer of Hebrews tells us that Jesus continues to be the praying Christ in heaven, since as the risen

Christ He has "a permanent priesthood" and connects His prayers with our safety and assurance of heaven (Hebrews 7:24–25). Thus the praying church on earth is linked to the praying Christ in heaven, the church in the storm with the Christ on the throne.

I once read of an old Victorian picture that illustrated this in a striking way. The artist had painted a famous gospel scene, the storm on the Sea of Galilee, in which Jesus comes to the terrified disciples, walking on the water. However, he had depicted the scene at an earlier stage, and at first all the observer could see was the lashing rain and the heaving waves of the storm-tossed lake, and the frightened disciples desperately rowing their threatened boat in the foreground. Only after a more careful examination could one see a human figure kneeling in prayer among the rocks of the hills bordering the lake. So, too, His people today are struggling, wrestling with the world, the flesh, and the Devil. He says to us, as He said to Peter, "I have prayed for you, that your faith might not fail." So our prayers meet His prayers; we are not unheard and we are not alone, and we will not be given up to the storm.

NOTE

1. F. F. Bruce, *The Epistle of Paul to the Galatians* (Carlisle, England: Paternoster, 1982), 75, 76.

Chapter Forty-Three

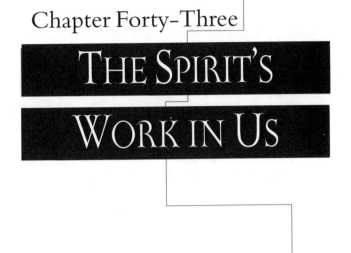

THE SPIRIT'S WORK IN US

The Holy Spirit's great desire and work is to make us like Christ, who is like God. It has been God's plan from the beginning that His chosen people (us!) might be "conformed to the likeness of his Son, that he might be the firstborn among many brothers" (Romans 8:29). As an indwelling Spirit, He has taken up His place at the center of our being, and from that center He exercises and extends His control (see Romans 8:9), isolating and attacking the sins that threaten us (Romans 8:13), and encouraging us by testifying with our spirits that we are God's children on the way to God's glory (Romans 8:16).

With Christ, the Holy Spirit works to deliver us from evil's power, helping us in our weakness and praying with us. He is our advocate and intercessor on earth, as Christ is our advocate and intercessor in heaven (Romans 8:26). It is thus that our Father in heaven takes us up into His purposes and into His life (Romans 8:27).

The prayer life of the Christian, like an outcrop of

rock on a green hillside, exposes the character and foundation of our lives. These lives of ours, so fragile, so vulnerable, so weak and unsatisfactory where the things of God are concerned, are, notwithstanding, lives that contain a great power, lives built upon a mighty foundation. Ours are lives that God has claimed as His own; our hearts are the place where Christ is being formed in us, "the hope of glory" (Colossians 1:27; cf. Galatians 4:19); our prayers are the oxygen of heaven which we often need to breathe amid the pollution of earth.

In that pollution many things flourish and grow that are inimical to the Christian life, and we are endangered by them. Hence our Lord, Himself wrestling with great temptation in Gethsemane and seeing His disciples unaware and so more vulnerable, warns them, "Watch and pray so that you will not fall into temptation" (Mark 14:38). The Holy Spirit makes our prayer life a poisonous atmosphere for Satan and a disinfectant for sin. Sin and prayer cannot live together; each is death to the other. As an old Puritan preacher put it: "Either praying will make you leave off sinning or sinning will make you leave off praying."[1] Thus when the apostle Paul is describing the Christian warfare and its armor, he ends his list of weapons with prayer: "And pray in the Spirit . . . with all kinds of prayers and requests. With this in mind . . . keep on praying for all the saints" (Ephesians 6:18).

The Holy Spirit works with similar effect when we read Holy Scripture. He makes the Word of God to be not only information but inspiration and power as we read it (see 2 Timothy 3:16–17). He enlarges our perspective, encourages our resolve, strengthens our faith. Even as we read, the words often come with a certain power and conviction into our minds and hearts. Again it is the Spirit working, working with the Word that He inspired in the first place; for He first gave it for people like you and me, and for you and me among them! It is our book—His and ours—a letter from home, in which our heavenly Father keeps in touch with us in our earthly travels and trials. It is the history of His mighty acts in our world, the record of the grand redemption achieved by the Son He sent into our world. It is the sound of His voice in our world today, penetrating the static of conflicting philosophies and rising above the chorus of contradictory claims.

As "the sword of the Spirit" (Ephesians 6:17), it is still an essential part of "the full armor of God" with which we can "take [our] stand against the devil's schemes" (Ephesians 6:11). It compels us to examine ourselves, our lives, their effect, and our very motives (Hebrews 4:12–13), and it does so in order that no one will fall on his or her way to God's rest (Hebrews 4:1–2). In a world of temptation to sin, of pressure to conform, of many opportunities but few securities, the believer needs a sure word to guide and to warn. Susannah Wesley, mother of John Wesley, gave her son a Bible to take with him to Oxford and his studies there. The university was not known for high words or great piety; John's brother, Charles, was to describe it after his own studies there as a place "where learning keeps its loftiest seat and hell its firmest throne!" Knowing that the great university was the graveyard of many a young man's faith and morality, Susannah wrote in the flyleaf: "Sin will keep you from this Book; but this Book will keep you from sin."

The Holy Spirit is not only at work in us; by the

same token He is at work in the believers around us, and they are a main part of our protection and comfort when hard times come. Christ not only draws people to Himself in every age, He also gathers us together in communities. The New Testament places great emphasis on the church as the purchased people of God, and not only on the universal church but on the local church: the believing community in covenant with God and one another. Christ has given the Holy Spirit to the churches to equip them with His gifts and graces, not only for witness in the world but for their mutual encouragement and strengthening in faith and holiness. The New Testament does not see us growing mature in Christ in isolation but in community, in the fellowship of the Holy Spirit (see 1 Corinthians 12:7; 2 Corinthians 13:14).

Here we carry one another's burdens (see Galatians 6:1–2) and surround one another in the protection of prayer and the encouragement of friendship. Here we surround each other in the atmosphere of true spiritual worship and counsel one another in the wisdom God gives generously and to all. Here we see in the ordinances and sing in the songs and hear in the preaching the great realities that have gripped us, the mighty love that has found us, and the blood-bought right of Jesus to be our Lord and King, our Savior and our Guide.

It is *together* we can become strong and wise without thereby becoming conceited and hard (see Romans 12:3, 9–16). It is *together* our light shines out into the world, bright and warm. It is *together* we can resist and defeat Satan, our great enemy. He might easily pick us off one by one in solitariness but not in "the fellowship of kindred minds." And in the last great day, when Christ our champion comes to vindicate His waiting church, then together the God of peace will crush Satan under our feet. (See 1 Thessalonians 4:13–19; Romans 16:20; 1 Corinthians 6:2–3.)

NOTE

1. Thomas Brooks, "The Privy Key of Heaven," vol. 11, *The Works of Thomas Brooks* (Edinburgh: Banner of Truth, 1980).

PART SIX

"FOR YOURS IS THE KINGDOM
AND THE POWER
AND THE GLORY FOREVER. AMEN"

Chapter Forty-Four

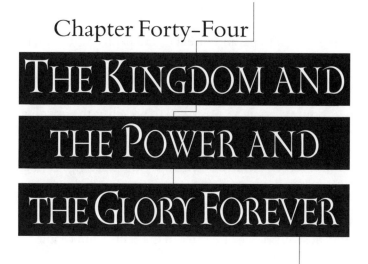

THE KINGDOM AND THE POWER AND THE GLORY FOREVER

*I*t is true that the final phrase of the Lord's Prayer may not have been an original part of the prayer as Jesus gave it. Scholars generally agree that the manuscript tradition is weighted in favor of omission. Yet it is equally clear that the church from very early times has added it and used it in her prayers and liturgies.[1] Its parts are taken from various Old Testament texts (for example, 1 Chronicles 29:11; Nehemiah 9:5; Psalm 145:12) and are wholly suitable to this New Testament prayer. It is, therefore, an addition that tells us something reliable about God and also something typical about the people who pray the prayer that Jesus gave them.

This is a prayer that ends in praise. The church's final statement is adoration, pure and simple. She gives herself up to doxology; the struggles of faith, the trials of hope, the losses and the gains of life all take second place to this. It is the true worshiper's final resting place. Yet in this too we express the three greatest and most abiding things: faith, hope, and love. For the people of God will always be a people of praise.

| YOURS IS THE KINGDOM

Some years ago I was asked to preach at the opening of a new church in Doncaster, England. The crowd coming was too great to fit inside the church, so the center of Doncaster Museum was rented for the opening service. Doncaster was an important garrison town in the days of the Roman occupation of Britain, and its large museum houses many relics of those days. The people gathered in the museum's large open area in the center, and I came to the front to preach the sermon.

I still vividly remember looking beyond the congregation to the scene surrounding us. I noticed the armor, the standards, and the weaponry of the Roman legions, and the signs of Roman pomp and glory—all in *glass cases.* And *here* were the once-despised Christians, the spiritual descendants of the martyrs of the arena, singing with joy and confidence the praises of our God and His Christ. Caesar was nothing, the legionaries of the great Roman Empire were nothing, they were dead figures of a dead past; but Jesus Christ was alive and powerfully at work in the world, gathering His people into an eternal kingdom and glory:

> So be it, Lord; Thy throne shall never,
> Like earth's proud empires, pass away;
> Thy kingdom stands and grows for ever,
> Till all Thy creatures own Thy sway.[2]

To be part of that kingdom is a greater privilege than the Caesars of yesterday or presidents and prime ministers of today can ever bestow. Only the reigning Christ who will judge the world will have the power to say of the kingdom in its full glory, to those who have followed Him: "Come, you who are blessed by my Father; take your inheritance, the kingdom prepared for you since the creation of the world" (Matthew 25:34). To have a place in this kingdom is a privilege as endless as it is incomparable, for "the righteous will shine like the sun in the kingdom of their Father" (Matthew 13:43).

YOURS IS THE POWER

We know something of power these days. Astronomers tell us that our sun is 500 times the mass of our earth and is like a vast hydrogen bomb burning slow-ly. Every second, four million tons of hydrogen are destroyed in explosions near the core. There, at the core, the heat is so intense that a pinhead of material would give off enough heat to kill a human being a million miles away. In one second it emits more energy than man has used up from the earth's resources since history began. Yet all of that is less than the striking of a match compared to the power of the God we know and love and serve. The colossal energies of the Big Bang and the expanding universe are no adequate measure of His power; they are but the overflow of His reserves, "the outskirts of His ways."

The power extolled here, however, is not the power that sustains creation but the power that directs it to a prepared end. It is God's sovereignty in providence and in grace, which is the bedrock of biblical religion and the immovable foundation of faith (see Isaiah 46:9–10).

Often that power is a hidden power, forging a path

through confusion, darkness, and storm in a fallen, god-less world, choosing the weak things of the world to shame the strong. It is the power of Christ, who is the power and wisdom of God (see 1 Corinthians 1:20–29). In the Gospels where the sick are healed and even the dead raised, glimpses of that power are revealed, and glimpses too of the new earth it will create, where every vestige and effect of the Fall will be erased. That same power is at work today even when the body is dead "because of sin," where sickness defeats us for a while (Romans 8:10). Even where death by martyrdom comes with no visible rescue, faith sees a Christ who has "the power of an indestructible life," seated at the right hand of God "far above all rule and authority, power and dominion" (Hebrews 7:16; Ephesians 1:21), a coming Christ waiting to vindicate our trust.

The last enemy that shall be destroyed is death (see Daniel 12:2). The power that opens the graves on the last day, the power that will raise glorified bodies for the already glorified souls of believers, is the power of God who raised Christ Jesus as our head. For Christ has been raised from the dead as "the firstfruits of those who have fallen asleep" (1 Corinthians 15:20; note also vv. 50–57). This is the "incomparably great power" of God, which is vested in Jesus Christ and which is already at work in we who believe. Thus Paul can give his blessing to the Ephesian Christians in these words: "Now to him who is able to do immeasurably more than all we ask or imagine, according to his power that is at work within us, to him be glory in the church and in Christ Jesus throughout all generations, for ever and ever! Amen" (Ephesians 3:20–21).

YOURS IS THE GLORY

You and I gasp at the glory of a sunset, marvel at the structure of a crystal, absorb the wonder of a landscape, and have a sense of glory from what is created. Or perhaps we hear a symphony or a sonata, see a painting or read out a poem, and have a sense of glory in what we ourselves create from the structures of sound, or observe in the brilliant and varied colors in God's world. We watch with respect, perhaps even awe, the pomp and occasion of a major public event. Take all these things and multiply their beauty or their brilliance, their depth of complexity or their height of perfection a thousand million times, and you will still have only a faint sense of the glory of God. For if there is all this beauty outside God, how much beauty there must be in the being of God.

In the Old Testament, the glory of God appeared in a unique way as an aura of dazzling light: it was called the *Kabod Yahweh,* the glory of God. Those who saw it could hardly describe it, and it left them feeling utterly weak and overawed and even prostrate. (See, for example, Ezekiel 1:25–2:1.) Such a demonstration of glory was meant to show the utter incomparability of God not only in majesty but also in purity, not only in power but also in goodness and righteousness and justice. (See Exodus 33:18–23; 34:5–7; Isaiah 6:1, 5.) His glory must not be given to any other being or power in the universe. He alone is God, and there is and will be no other (see Isaiah 42:8; 48:11).

It is all the more startling, therefore, to find throughout the New Testament the honors of Yahweh being shared with Jesus in forgiving sins, in judging the world, in receiving the honors and worship due to God and the name that is divine (see Mark 2:10; John 5:22–23; Philippians 2:9–11). Moreover, Jesus Himself is described in terms of His preexistent life in the Godhead as "the radiance of God's glory" (Hebrews 1:3). In the words of one of the church's greatest confessions, He is and ever was:

> God of God,
> Light of Light,
> true God of true God,
> begotten not made,
> of one substance with the Father.[3]

In His earthly life, the incarnate Son lived for the glory of God; in His exalted life, the glorified Son shares the glory of God. Now the kingdom is His and the power is His and the glory is His. It is a glory He alone can share because He enjoyed with the Father equal glory before the world began (see John 16:14–15; 17:1, 5). It is a glory Saul of Tarsus saw streaming as dazzling light from the face of the Nazarene, and he knew they had crucified the Lord of glory (see Acts 9:3–5; 26:13–15).

Yet into the blessing of that glory we are called; for, as much as we creatures can do, we too shall share the glory (see Romans 8:18; Philippians 3:21), which Christ has purchased for us by His death and holds for us in His endless resurrection life. So Paul urges the Thessalonians and us "to live lives worthy of God, who calls you into his kingdom and glory" (1 Thessalonians 2:12).

For almost 2,000 years the followers of Christ have repeated this "Lord's Prayer" and have sealed it with this final statement. In the mouths of believers everywhere and in all conditions, it has expressed the presence of the great triad: "faith, hope, and love" (1 Corinthians 13:13). It has been a statement of faith, an expression of hope, and a declaration of love. Let's look at how this benediction declares our faith, hope, and love; and with these three things we end our study of this prayer.

| A STATEMENT OF FAITH

What is faith? It is not easy to define faith as such. It is hard for faith to explain itself. This is not at all surprising, for the content of faith is its object and not itself; the thing believed rather than the act of believing. Faith finds virtue only in its object, God: His existence, His character, His Word, His mighty acts in the biblical history, and now, above all, in His only Son our Lord Jesus Christ, incarnate, crucified, risen, and exalted. This is the way faith lives, not striving to will something into existence but resting on something God has brought into existence: His kingdom, His power, His glory made known to us and shared with us in the Gospel of Jesus Christ.

Faith then is *believing God,* recognizing and receiving His revelation of Himself and His truth, and committing ourselves to Him for this life and the next, for time and eternity.

Faith—true faith, saving faith—has specific content. It is neither mysticism nor gullibility nor a generous open-mindedness. As John Stott puts it, "Faith is not a synonym for credulity or superstition. . . . Faith is a reasonable trust."[4] It is based on the historic events of the gospel, not on a suprahistorical mythology or a cloudy supernaturalism. Above all, it is based upon the reliability of Jesus: His claims, His offer of forgiveness, and His promise of eternal life. It is through Him that we enter the kingdom of God. It is He who is the power of God for salvation.

It is faith's triumph that in a world of contradiction and contention it can look to the God and Father of our Lord Jesus Christ and say, "Yours is the kingdom and the power and the glory forever. Amen."

AN EXPRESSION OF HOPE

The doxology at the end of the Lord's Prayer leaves us looking upward and also looking forward to a God of undefeatable purpose, of unequaled power and eternal glory. It is a final note of defiance to the forces of darkness and of confidence in the God who is Light, who is above all and over all, blessed forever (see Romans 9:5; 11:36; Ephesians 4:6). The biblical word for such confidence is *hope*. In common use today, hope is a synonym for uncertainty, as in the statement: "We hope for good weather during our holidays." In the New Testament use of the word, however, hope has a quite different meaning. It signifies confident expectation, strong assurance, and it is never tinged with nervousness or alarm, as so often in secular contexts.

The character and dominance of hope was a striking feature of early Christian faith in contrast to much philosophy and religious thought. One scholar writes: "Living hope as a fundamental religious attitude was unknown in Greek culture. . . . In the final analysis men had to stand without hope before the hostile forces of guilt and death."[5] We see much of that today, too, and it has been a very dominant feature of much popular post-war philosophy, leading to cynicism and despair.

Saul Bellow writes graphically of this in the novel *Herzog:* "This generation thinks—and this is its thoughts—that nothing faithful, vulnerable, fragile can be durable or have any true power. Death waits for these things as a cement floor waits for a dropping light bulb."[6]

As a typical Woody Allen line puts it, "The future is not what it used to be." But that is just what the believer denies as he or she ends prayer with such words as these. The future is still *precisely* what it used to be, because God is unchanging in His character, purposes, promises, and power: "I the Lord do not change. So you, O descendants of Jacob, are not destroyed"; and because "Jesus Christ is the same yesterday and today and forever" (Malachi 3:6; Hebrews 13:8).

Christ has come, Christ has died, Christ is risen, Christ is coming again:

> . . . and therein lies all hope on the Christian view. For hope is not a mere refusal to accept defeat, a heroic virtue to be mustered and maintained by noble souls in the face of suffering, disaster, despair, or even of life's mere drudgery. Much less is it an attitude of general optimism to be cultivated from, by and for itself. It is the response of joy that flashes to life in anyone who sees what Christ's coming means, like the thrill that comes to haggard clumps of war prisoners who see the camp gates suddenly crashing inward and their own troops arriving.[7]

It is with such hope that faith sees that day approaching and a pilgrim church daily affirms, "Yours is the (incoming) kingdom and the (unfailing) power and the (approaching) glory."

A DECLARATION OF LOVE

The "amen" at the end of the prayer is a form of an old Hebrew word that indicates certainty and dependability. It was used to confirm a statement made by someone else or as a response that acknowledged the validity and binding nature of an agreement. As such, it is like a personal signature, involving ourselves in what has been said. It could be translated "so be it" or "I agree" or "surely it is so." Jesus unusually, perhaps uniquely, used it at the beginning rather than the end of some of His sayings to authorize them as certain and reliable, to make them binding on His followers, and as an expression of His own majesty and authority.

In the mouths of God's willing people, however, and in the mouths of His children who pray the Lord's Prayer, the *amen* is a final note of love and self-giving. For the kingdom is His—and yet He has shared it with us. And the power is His—which might have crushed us but which has caught us "in the ambush of an infinite and everlasting love surrounding us without the possibility of escape from it."[8] And the glory is His—a glory that might have been forever forbidden us, leaving us exiled in unending darkness. But with matchless grace and marvelous generosity, He calls us into His glory and makes it the inheritance of all believers (see Colossians 1:12–13; Jude 24).

In view of such things, and in view of their cost at Calvary, how can our final amen be anything other than an amen of self-giving love, in response to God's self-giving love? Thus Isaac Watts declares in the final verse of "When I Survey the Wondrous Cross":

Were the whole realm of nature mine,
That were a present far too small;
Love so amazing, so divine,
Demands my life, my soul, my all.[9]

NOTES

1. J. Jeremias writes: "According to contemporary analogies Jesus must have intended that the Our Father should conclude with a doxology, but would have left the user to fill it in for himself." Quoted in Leon Morris, *The Gospel According to Matthew* (Grand Rapids: Eerdmans, 1992), 149.
2. John Ellerton (1826–93), "The Day Thou Gavest, Lord, Is Ended." In public domain.
3. Extract from the Creed of Nicea, A.D. 325.
4. John Stott quoted in Russell Chandler, *Understanding the New Age* (Dallas: Word, 1988).
5. E. Hoffmann in *The New International Dictionary of New Testament Theology,* vol. 2 (Exeter, England: Paternoster, 1976), 239.
6. Saul Bellow, *Herzog,* quoted in Millard J. Ericksen, *Christian Theology* (Grand Rapids: Baker, 1986), 1065.
7. J. I. Packer and Thomas Howard, *Christianity: The True Humanism* (Waco, Tex.: Word, 1985), 95.
8. Thomas Goodwin (1600–1680), *The Work of the Holy Ghost in Our Salvation* (Edinburgh: James Nichol, 1863 reprint), 144.
9. Isaac Watts (1674–1748), "When I Survey the Wondrous Cross." In public domain.

REVIEW AND STUDY GUIDE

INTRODUCTION

*T*he purpose of the Foundations of the Faith series is to reacquaint the reader with some of the great doctrines and favorite Scripture passages relating to our Christian life. Indeed, these books attempt to link together our faith as we understand it and our life as we live it. Though our goal is to provide more in-depth teaching on a topic, we hope to accomplish this with a popular style and practical application. Books in the series include the Lord's Prayer, the Ten Commandments, Psalm 23, and 1 Corinthians 13.

In keeping with our goal of a popular-level treatment, this review and study guide is not meant to involve exhaustive digging, but to reinforce the important concepts in the "Points to Consider" and to help you explore some of their implications in the "Questions and Response."

A book's impact is judged in the long term, and if you can retain at least one important point per chapter and answer and act upon some of the questions relevant to your life, you have made considerable progress. May God bless your walk with Him as you enter into these exercises.

JAMES S. BELL, JR.

PART ONE

"OUR FATHER IN HEAVEN, HALLOWED BE YOUR NAME"

Points to Consider

CHAPTER ONE

1. The Father loves us unconditionally, delighting in us continually, even though we are unworthy sinners.

2. Regardless of the performance of your earthly father, God wants a relationship that will not deny you the perfect Father love.

CHAPTER TWO

1. A God who is able to be great in the big things—who is able to create the universe—can excel in the small things too.

2. Don't focus your attention on the achievements of humanity but on the majesty of God.

CHAPTER THREE

1. God's glory is beautiful beyond description but terrifying because we are unclean.

2. Praise God, we can enter His presence with safety and confidence.

CHAPTER FOUR

1. God is in complete control—of our challenges, problems, and circumstances.

2. We need not be fearful because His invisible presence is always at our side to protect us.

Chapter Five

1. Though we need to be reverent and humble, we are made one with the Father and may address Him in familiar terms.

2. Our great High Priest, Jesus Christ, gives us the assurance and confidence we need to approach Him.

Chapter Six

1. God expresses His holiness primarily through self-giving love, especially in the gift to us of His only Son.

2. God could have destroyed His creation and started over, but He entered into a "holy conspiracy" to perfect what He began.

Chapter Seven

1. God has a plan for our lives and promises to steer us in the right direction in order to fulfill it.

2. The actual choices in our decision making are not as important as the attitude, motivation, and consecration behind them.

Chapter Eight

1. When we surrender to God's authority we are the most free—both from the effects of sin and the need for discipline.

2. Our obedience is not begrudging or a mere acknowledgment of right, but stems from love and gratefulness.

CHAPTER NINE

1. Without the Father's loving connection and discipline, we would naturally follow our own selfish and rebellious ways.

2. As we live out our faith in the world we are challenged to compromise, and God's discipline keeps us on the narrow path.

CHAPTER TEN

1. The Father shows His direct, personal love not just through faith but at times through direct experience through the Holy Spirit.

2. God's love can be felt as serene and sweet, or as passionate and explosive, and we feel as if we can take no more.

CHAPTER ELEVEN

1. Ethical absolutes are not abstract concepts but linked to the character of God, doable because we are His children.

2. We can imitate God because He gave us His Son as an example to be applied in our family life and other spheres of influence.

Chapter Twelve

1. In our secular Western culture the focus on ourselves has failed, and people now seek the spiritual side of life through different religions.

2. Worship should rise to the heights of pure adoration as we realize that we can actually please the almighty God with our homage.

Chapter Thirteen

1. Serving God does not mean withdrawing from the world, but zealously fulfilling your calling there, serving with excellence.

2. Your beliefs as a child of God need to be lived out in the world, challenging the assumptions of the world and transforming it.

Chapter Fourteen

1. Our natural inclination is to view ourselves as righteous, but self-centeredness and pride have blinded us regarding our true state.

2. As we revere God's name rather than our own, we find our true home with the Father as well as our rightful inheritance.

Questions and Responses

1. God's sovereignty, or absolute rule in our lives, should not be intimidating, but comforting. Why? (Chapter 4)

2. In seeking God's guidance, the decision might be correct but God still may not be pleased. How does motivation play a role? (Chapter 7)

3. Review the experiences of the Holy Spirit of Edwards, Moody, Wesley, etc. When have you felt the love of God who delights in you? (Chapter 10)

4. The author writes, "A sight of God is a breathtaking thing." Identify three of your own "God-sightings" when you were swept away by His presence and power. (Chapter 12)

5. What does it mean to deny the centrality of your self-life rather than some pleasure or bad habit? What is it about our own nature that wants to be in the place of God? (Chapter 14)

PART TWO

"YOUR KINGDOM COME,
YOUR WILL BE DONE
ON EARTH AS IT IS IN HEAVEN"

Points to Consider

CHAPTER FIFTEEN

1. We are our own worst enemies. Even with the best intentions for a moral society, we fail, and only God can remove the evil from us.

2. All the world's achievements will come to nothing in the end —only what is done for Christ and His kingdom will endure.

CHAPTER SIXTEEN

1. Salvation history is the process of God calling a specific people to be set apart in every way from all the other nations.

2. God intervened in human history to establish His kingly reign. The King Himself will come again to finalize this.

CHAPTER SEVENTEEN

1. Jesus brought in a kingdom of liberation, mercy, and peace— not primarily of judgment or vengeance.

2. Today we live in between kingdoms, with the final fulfillment of the rule of Christ still to come.

Chapter Eighteen

1. The church must live out kingdom life, modeling a community of reconciled people who care for and are committed to each other.

2. The coming of the kingdom will bring great joy to some and terror to others, and it will be a final, irreversible separation.

Chapter Nineteen

1. Though we need protection from the "pollution" of the world, isolation would not allow us to fulfill our kingdom agenda.

2. Our role in this world is paradoxical—building up and destroying, comforting and criticizing, warming and wooing.

Chapter Twenty

1. The church has advanced greatly in numbers since the first century, but we are often soft and ineffective in our mission.

2. God gives us power to use, especially to share the gospel with others, providing us with unique opportunities and circumstances.

CHAPTER TWENTY-ONE

1. The most perfect prayer is that God's will be done because it cuts out our own selfish interests and the ignorance of His ways.

2. Placing God's will above ours does not restrict us but gives us the greatest freedom to reach our own unique potential.

CHAPTER TWENTY-TWO

1. God's sovereignty takes over when other principles of guidance don't seem to work. He always honors our biblical approach.

2. His ways will inevitably at times lead us down difficult paths, but He is always in control and will lead us to joy.

CHAPTER TWENTY-THREE

1. Surrendering our will takes huge effort, but God's acting grace is sufficient for the task of changing our thinking, acting, and living.

2. Discipleship means listening, believing, following, and responding to the master, whatever the cost.

Chapter Twenty-Four

1. Human needs are not the ultimate purpose of our lives nor should their fulfillment constitute our identity. Rather, our purpose comes in what we give.

2. Our lives are, in effect, a little bit of heaven for the world to see as we demonstrate the love of Christ to one another.

Chapter Twenty-Five

1. Christ actually enjoyed obeying the Father, even though the mission entailed deep suffering, because of His deep love for the Father and for us.

2. Christ is the only one to experience the two extremes of existence, both the depths of humanity and the heights of exaltation.

Questions and Responses

1. In terms of the kingdom of God, how can you as a Christian live the future in the present? In what ways is the kingdom of God now and not yet? (Chapter 17)

2. Why is it necessary for God to exclude the unrighteous from heaven in order to obtain joy in the kingdom for His chosen ones? How should this future separation affect your desire to evangelize now? (Chapter 18)

3. If we cannot be successfully independent from God and His will, how can we experience true individuality and freedom? (Chapter 21)

4. Name at least four important steps in seeking God's guidance in your decisions. If we are still unsure, how can we be confident? (Chapter 22)

5. How does obedience to Jesus satisfy your true needs (rather than certain felt needs) even if such obedience is difficult or even painful? (Chapter 24)

PART THREE

"GIVE US TODAY
OUR DAILY BREAD"

Points to Consider

CHAPTER TWENTY-SIX

1. If we do not pray for something and yet expect God to give it to us anyway, we are guilty of presumption and/or self-sufficiency.

2. Giving God His due glory comes first in prayer before requests that focus on our needs.

CHAPTER TWENTY-SEVEN

1. God has promised to meet our needs and not necessarily our wants. Thus our focus in petition should be on spiritual needs first.

2. To some people prayer may seem like an escape from responsibility, but it actually transforms us, if not our circumstances as well.

CHAPTER TWENTY-EIGHT

1. God cares. He suffers along with us in the results of our fallenness and rebellion toward Him, but this is especially true at the Cross.

2. God does not cause evil or watch indifferently but rather works all things to the good according to His plan and provision.

Chapter Twenty-Nine

1. We should not seek contentment from resources that are outside our control or that will not last, because they will fail us.

2. We should not be indifferent upon receiving material success and goods, but should be content whether we have such success or not.

Chapter Thirty

1. Poverty is not a necessary state for the Christian, but its related values of simplicity, generosity, and contentment are very important.

2. Our service to those less fortunate may affect only one person, but for that person it's all the difference in the world.

Questions and Responses

1. Why must God Himself take precedence over our needs and troubles, even during great trials? How does He come along and meet our concerns when He is first? (Chapter 26)

2. How does anxiety over such things as money or health, if allowed to get out of hand, compare to a type of atheism? How does prayer keep us from this obsession? If you have felt anxiety recently and not brought that concern to the Father, do so now. Confess your lack of trust and praise Him for His sovereign plan in your life. (Chapter 27)

3. God's sovereignty remains in a world of senseless evil and pain. How does His providential care utilize disappointment and failure in our lives? (Chapter 28)

4. Why does knowing how little we deserve and how much we have been forgiven help us to be content with the basics in life? (Chapter 29)

5. In light of the complete self-giving of Christ, what should be our response to those less fortunate? Do we practice simplicity, generosity, and contentment so that others may benefit as well? Evaluate what you have done recently in these areas and what you can do in the future. (Chapter 30)

PART FOUR

"FORGIVE US OUR DEBTS
AS WE ALSO HAVE
FORGIVEN OUR DEBTORS"

Points to Consider

CHAPTER THIRTY-ONE

1. One generation's sins can affect their children and can increase the negative repercussions over time if there is no repentance.

2. We are debtors not because God is being difficult but because we have misused His gifts and rebelled against His commands.

CHAPTER THIRTY-TWO

1. If God's initial forgiveness were not sufficient, we would be in constant anxiety regarding present and future sins disqualifying us.

2. What causes us to both greatly love and forgive is the fact that Christ first loved and forgave us even though we did not deserve it.

CHAPTER THIRTY-THREE

1. Repentance is a radical turning away from our old life to follow God's path, yet it is a gift because we cannot do it ourselves.

2. We do not have to wait until the final Judgment Day to hear our personal verdict, but we can know now that God has justified us by faith.

Chapter Thirty-Four

1. Pardon from God is the only power that can dramatically change a life, because He gives us a fresh start free from the effects of our sins.

2. In light of the Cross all of our excuses, self-justification, cynicism, and doubt melt away. He has died for our sins and thus has overcome the power of sin.

Chapter Thirty-Five

1. The Holy Spirit is always within us, but we need to keep in step with His activity if we are to fully utilize His power.

2. We should pity rather than resent those who have offended us and forgive them because they have offended God and will pay for it.

Questions and Responses

1. What process takes place whereby gifts we receive from God become "bad debts" we cannot repay? How do we misuse what we do not deserve? (Chapter 31)

2. What is the worst form of chastisement God administers when we have not sought forgiveness for sins? Why is it harder than direct punishment? (Chapter 32)

3. Repentance is a change of mind, heart, and life. How have these three changes worked together in one particular area of your own life? (Chapter 33)

4. How does the power of pardon change you? What do you lose and what do you gain when you repent of past sins? (Chapter 34)

5. How does Satan make sin attractive and then condemn us for it? How can you stand against him when dealing with those who have offended you? (Chapter 35)

PART FIVE

"AND LEAD US NOT
INTO TEMPTATION,
BUT DELIVER US
FROM THE EVIL ONE"

Points to Consider

CHAPTER THIRTY-SIX

1. God does not tempt us to sin, but He does test our faith to draw us closer, prove His commitment, and turn us around to help others.

2. Strong temptations can be a blessing, because they can make us aware of the extreme danger we face without God's protection.

CHAPTER THIRTY-SEVEN

1. We often feel that God is angry with us when we undergo trials, but He wants to mature, refine, and develop His own people.

2. Extreme testing, such as persecution, brings out our true character, especially our weaknesses, but at the same time it purifies and strengthens.

CHAPTER THIRTY-EIGHT

1. Our reason and our passions battle each other, and they make us complex beings who are easily influenced by evil in its subtle forms.

2. Satan's main focus of attack is God Himself. In trying to thwart God's plan for the church, Satan hopes to stop His eternal purposes.

Chapter Thirty-Nine

1. In a damaged world we can sometimes miss the evidence of God's working, yet we can look to the promises that say restoration will occur in the end.

2. Our faith must lead to understanding worked out in obedience. If it remains in the intellect alone, it leads back to doubt.

Chapter Forty

1. Our culture has an obsession with sex that spills into the church, causing the breakdown of the family as well as personal morality.

2. It's important to work on temptations with your spouse early on, as well as to develop intimacy to protect the marital bond.

Chapter Forty-One

1. Learn what category of Christian you fit into—new, strategic, older, or worldly Christian—and it will help you understand how Satan tempts you in your vulnerable spots.

2. Weaknesses are our danger zones, and we should stay as far removed from those situations, thoughts, or even people as is possible.

Chapter Forty-Two

1. Christ has set us free from much cruel slavery: our flesh, our sin, the Devil, and the spirit of the evil age in which we live.

2. Our salvation was won by Christ while He was on earth, but even now He continues to intercede for us in our daily struggles with the world, flesh, and Devil.

Chapter Forty-Three

1. The Holy Spirit aids us in prayer and produces the breath of heaven in the poisonous sinful atmosphere of earth.

2. The work of the Spirit is not just in us as individuals, but working in the body of Christ to provide fellowship and a united witness to the world.

Questions and Responses

1. When have you faced a situation where God did not stop a trial when you thought you had learned the lesson? What did He accomplish after that point as you look back? (Chapter 37)

2. Two remedies for doubting are to increase the knowledge of your faith and to put what you have into practice. How might you do both in a practical way? (Chapter 39)

3. When is the most opportune time to deal with sexual temptation? Describe the step-by-step process when you eventually become overpowered and commit sin. (Chapter 40)

4. Based on the descriptions in chapter 41, what category of Christian are you—new, strategic, older, or worldly Christian? Knowing this, what are your likely vulnerable spots and what can you do to prepare for Satan's temptations in these areas?

5. How do the Holy Spirit and the Word of God work together to bring about growth in our lives? How do we, like John Wesley, use it to stand against the philosophies of the day? (Chapter 43)

PART SIX

"FOR YOURS IS THE KINGDOM
AND THE POWER
AND THE GLORY FOREVER. AMEN"

Points to Consider

1. The greatest visible sign of the power of God will be when our bodies are raised to life from the grave on the last day, when death will be defeated.

2. The doxology to the Lord's Prayer is an expression of hope: the future arrival of His kingdom, by His power which never fails, and the revelation of His glory.

Questions and Responses

1. Write down your own definition of faith in the context of the following three terms: rest, hope, and trust. What other aspects of faith can you think of? (Chapter 44)

2. When we say "amen" we commit ourselves to the truths of the Lord's Prayer. Name three things you will do to lovingly serve God in response to these truths.